INSIDE
WAKEFIELD
PRISON

INSIDE WAKEFIELD PRISON

Life Behind Bars in the Monster Mansion

JONATHAN LEVI & EMMA FRENCH

jb

First published in the UK by John Blake Publishing
An imprint of The Zaffre Publishing Group
A Bonnier Books UK company
4th Floor, Victoria House
Bloomsbury Square,
London, WC1B 4DA
England

Owned by Bonnier Books
Sveavägen 56, Stockholm, Sweden

www.facebook.com/johnblakebooks
twitter.com/jblakebooks

First published in paperback in 2024

Paperback ISBN: 978-1-78946-753-6
Ebook ISBN: 978-1-78946-754-3
Audiobook ISBN: 978-1-78946-755-0

British Library Cataloguing-in-Publication Data:

A catalogue record for this book is available from the British Library.

Design by www.envydesign.co.uk

Printed and bound in Great Britain by Clays Ltd, Elcograf S.p.A.

3 5 7 9 10 8 6 4

John Blake Publishing is an imprint of Bonnier Books UK
www.bonnierbooks.co.uk

*'I always look behind me since
I worked in Wakefield'*

JO TAYLOR

Contents

Prologue

There would be plenty of time for questions later. Right now, on a wild day in 2013, some very rough justice was about to be handed out to one of Wakefield's newest arrivals, paedophile child killer Mark Bridger, by two exceptionally dangerous men. We let one of them tell their own story, never told before, of what happened.

I was serving a whole life so therefore had nothing to lose. Mark Bridger, who murdered April Jones, was located on my wing. On the exercise yard the gangs were planning to attack him. The Muslims said they would and I was asked with Juvinal Ferreira to carry out the attack. I used nail clippers to take the top of a can off. I inserted two razors into the lid and bent it around the base of the razors to hold them in place. A handle. I used a table leg as a hammer. I taped up the handle. I made two of them.

The Sunday morning, I told the Muslims and other gang members to complete all their cooking in the morning because I knew the wing would be locked down in the afternoon as it would be a crime scene. On the afternoon Bridger was sitting on a chair outside a man's cell. I put him in a head lock and pulled him in the cell. We both fell on a bed. Ferreira and I cut him. He had his throat cut and a wound from his forehead around his eye down his cheek to his throat. It was horrendous. I was smothered in blood and staff chased me and Ferreira from the cell.

I ran to my cell, but staff knowing I had a razor refused to come in but locked me in the cell. I put my hand down the toilet under the u-bend and flushed the razor. Police later searched the outside drains but never got the weapon. The wing was locked down and police came on the wing and sealed it off and took photos. Later that night prison officers came to my door with full kit on and took me handcuffed, Ferreira, Ali and McCarry to the segregation unit.

I was held there for months, I spent over a year in segregation over this. I was in a cell with nothing. A concrete base for a bed, a fire blanket. A cardboard-made chair and table. I was assessed for CSC [closed supervised centre conditions]. It was here I met Charles Bronson who I hated. I will come to him later. The police were involved.

Ferreira was paid £700 to plead guilty to it. He was serving a thirty-year sentence and just received another life sentence. I claimed, 'Yes I was in the cell and Bridger just fell on me when they, Ferreira and him were wrestling.' My actions were appalling and this is still on my record some eleven years later. While I was never charged, and the fact Ferreira admitted it on interview – I never spoke – my prison record states I was responsible, put Ferreira up to it and I planned it. That happened in 2013 and to this day I am still considered high risk to other offenders and high risk to staff. Even though I have not offended violently in the past eleven years... That is an example of the gang culture and violence I signed up to. In hindsight looking back now, who was I to judge Bridger given my own crimes. For me then, given the dangerous environment I was in at HMP Wakefield, violence meant I was left alone. His injuries were horrendous and I truly regret it now. I am not that person now.

Major Contributors

Jo Taylor is a witty, down-to-earth woman, and as a straight-talking, 'firm but fair' former officer of both New Hall and Wakefield, she's seen it all having spent fifteen years in the service. She has great hair, as you might expect from someone who gave up a career in the prison service to conduct bespoke scalp micropigmentation treatments. Her airy, spacious and welcoming salon, with snacks, beverages, comfy chairs and a training table with model heads, enjoys an extraordinary view from her top-floor windows right over Wakefield Prison.

John Hartshorne is a self-disciplined former Wakefield officer who took up various roles after leaving the Royal Navy throughout his long career in the prison service. Kind-hearted and witty but professional, John knows all there is to know about the historic prison.

Pete Wightman is a veteran Wakefield staff member, a thickly set Yorkshireman, clean shaven with black glasses and short, dark hair. We were so grateful for his extraordinary stories. During one of our meetings, he had a picture of a deserted island behind him that lit up and played soothing sounds of the sea. 'I used to need things like that when I were working in the prison service.'

Geoffrey Wansell is a razor-sharp, forensic and charming true-crime writer, TV presenter and movie producer. He has spent decades researching the most notorious of crime cases, and has published many books including works on Fred and Rosemary West and Levi Bellfield. Extremely sprightly, Geoffrey shows no signs of slowing down, and was filming something about Levi Bellfield when we spoke to him, as well as doing a national tour in conversation with the renowned Poirot actor David Suchet.

Hayley Grocock is Chief Executive Officer of Wakefield District Sight Aid. A passionate and fiercely intelligent charity CEO, her work has taken her inside Wakefield, where the impact of the Braille work on the men there left an indelible impression on her.

'Jenny', as we will refer to her to protect her confidentiality, served three years and eight months in prison herself for conspiracy to supply class A drugs. She was happy to share her candid memories of her time inside. Being inside prison broke her dad's heart.

She turned her life around: she got counselling with her mum to fix their relationship and three years after getting out she now has a branch manager job. 'It was the best thing that ever happened to me.' She matured a lot and did a lot of work on herself.

Martin Baker brings a wealth of experience as an officer, and he is the kind of person you could just listen to all day. He joined Wakefield in 1999, intially as an SO in the PE department and progressing through promotions before going part time age sixty.

Vanessa Frake-Harris is a retired prison governor. She served twenty-seven years, 1986 to 2013, starting as an officer at Holloway and becoming Head of Operations and Security at Wormwood Scrubs in 2002. She is a seasoned officer not easily surprised or rattled, and has worked with some of the most notorious prisoners, male and female, throughout her time at Holloway and Wormwood Scrubs.

Paul and Lisa Powell, our dynamic duo, are a husband-and-wife team who fell in love working together at Wakefield and who shared the highs and lows of their experiences there. Paul joined the prison service in 1986 at Leeds, then Full Sutton, before Wakefield from 1993 to his 2014 retirement. During that time, he was an officer, then an SO and was temporarily promoted to a PO before he left. Lisa joined the prison service in 1987, and started at Wakefield in 1989. She finished as an Officer before retiring in 2013.

Robert Verkaik is a bestselling author whose gripping, meticulously researched books include *The Traitor of Colditz*. He spent an extraordinary two hours with Bronson and gave us exclusive details about the meeting.

Dr Maria Adams is an Associate Professor in Criminology at the University of Surrey. She is a well-respected academic who granted us vital insights into prison regime, food, and the broader impact of incarceration on families.

Michelle did not want us to disclose her surname, but she worked for the shoe-repair company Timpson for more than twenty years, and offered us some real insights into the company's extraordinary prison work.

Highly concerned about confidentiality and keen to avoid any sensationalism or publicity, the man we call '**Jim**' is drawn to the facts and doesn't take any nonsense. Used to visiting multiple prisons as someone who was involved at a high level in key operational aspects of the prison service, he has a well-rounded understanding, which has gained him respect throughout the service.

Introduction

Nicknamed 'Monster Mansion', HMP Wakefield has seen some of the most infamous prisoners of all time pass through its cells, from Levi Bellfield to Harold Shipman. Plenty of them are still in there. Today, the prison has the capacity, and the specialised security and facilities, for 750 of the country's most dangerous offenders, including Robert Maudsley, Michael Sams and Ian Watkins. Featuring the most sinister and shocking stories that have emerged from the prison, as well as new unheard tales, we take you inside Wakefield.

In addition to extraordinary staff stories and the insights of experts, crime writers and academics, we have truly explosive prisoner testimony. This book contains Wakefield in its prisoners' own words, something that has never been seen before.

What is it like arriving at Wakefield? We will let one of them describe it to you.

Entering HMP W [HMP Wakefield], the gates would open and the van carrying the prisoners would enter the air lock and stop. The air lock is an enclosed gated secure area between the outside [entrance] and the entrance to the prison grounds. The van would stop and the gates behind the van would close. OSG [Operational Support Grade, prison support worker] staff who are known as gate men would then check the van. They will enter the van and check the holding cells in the van. The van is subject to vigorous security checks, a mirror under the van, identification checked on all in the van, officers included. Holding warrants from the courts which relate to the prisoners and their dynamic risk assessment packs are checked. These packs as they are known are basically a file on the prisoner. His record and escape risk. Officers will then go through airport-type scanners and they will be searched. The prisoners will remain locked in their cell on the van while all this is taking place. This exercise would normally take about twenty minutes.

The officers on the escort will be issued keys to the prison and they will return onto the van. A dog man will then walk and escort the van into the prison to the reception area. The reception area at HMP is a short distance from the air-lock entrance. The gates will open and the van will enter at a slow pace. The reception area at HMP W is very small. The prisoner will be escorted off the van into the reception area. Finger-printed on the scanner and it will reveal instantly who the prisoner is. The prisoner is then uncuffed. Even during the journey all prisoners are handcuffed then locked in the small hold cell on the van. The prisoner is asked to walk through a body scanner X-ray type machine, strip-searched and again subject to further metal detectors [a wand]. The prisoner is given a fresh set of clothing to wear. A nurse will come to see the prisoner to check on the welfare.

This is normally a five-minute chat. Are you on any medication? Are you suicidal? Do you have any injuries? Do you have any mental health issues? Upon leaving the reception area at HMP W you are walked to the housing units [the wings]. Upon entering the wing, you will be locked in a cell until the following day. Meals would be a lunch pack. A roll, packet of crisps, a small drink and a tea pack – a small plastic bag which contains tea bags, milk powder and sugars.

Having written the hugely successful *Sunday Times* bestseller *Inside Broadmoor*, we knew that there was an appetite amongst our readers for getting the inside track on some of Britain's most renowned secure environments, inhabited by many of Britain's most dangerous men.

Although a couple of other prisons came close, HMP Frankland for instance, which Jonathan got to know though a recent TV documentary he made about Peter Sutcliffe, the Yorkshire Ripper, we felt that that HMP Wakefield should be our next focus.

Monster Mansion. A nickname that chills to the bone. Channel 5 is famous for its true-crime documentaries and when it transmitted a film about this institution it rated very well. It signalled to us there is massive public interest in the place and we felt determined to crack it, to get you inside, to connect you with the people that live and work there and find ways to tell you their untold stories.

Just thinking about the terrible things these incarcerated men have done fills us with admiration for the people who are prepared to work there, willing to devote their working lives to keeping the rest of us safe from this small but appalling section of our community. What these men have done is often viewed as evil, pure and simple. They are being punished, not treated. Yet as we got deeper into our story, the more we pondered appearance versus reality.

Many of us on the outside would see them as appalling but most people that work with long-serving prisoners get to know the human beneath the reputation. We have spoken to many people intimately connected with the place and we can share exclusive stories that have never been in the public domain. We also follow the prison's long and intriguing history from when it was first built in 1594 all the way up to the present day.

One of the most important things to us in our work as writers is to myth-bust, and to find the answers to the questions we know that everyone wants to know. What is the truth about Maudsley's segregation? Do the nonces and child killers really have a harder time than other inmates? Can the most notorious criminals ever be rehabilitated? Does it look like the prison we all have in our minds from the movies? How do they keep these highly dangerous men in line... and what happens when they step out of line?

One prisoner who contributed was equally keen to myth-bust and to offer himself as a unique witness; that said, he is also highly intelligent and manipulative, and his words must be taken in that context.

Dear sir, I hope the following helps you with your research into HMP Wakefield. It is rare and quite unique that you are given an honest insight into the prison from a person who spent many years there and witnessed much.

Chapter I

History of
HMP Wakefield

Wakefield's most recent prison inspection in 2022 gave a fascinating snapshot of the current make-up of the inmates. Hundreds of years after its foundation, today HMP Wakefield is a high-security prison for category A and B male prisoners, almost exclusively holding those with a determinate sentence of over ten years, lifers and prisoners with an indeterminate sentence for public protection.

Like most of the UK's prisons, Wakefield is virtually full. At that time there were 743 prisoners out of its 750 operational capacity. Amongst that number were an extraordinary 339 'life-sentenced prisoners' (over 45 per cent of the total prison population) and 36 prisoners 'serving an indeterminate sentence for public protection'. A horrifying 61 per cent of Wakefield's 2022 inmates had been convicted of a sexual offence. There had been

191 'receptions', or new arrivals, over the last year, but just 13 prisoners released into the community over the same time period. There were 67 foreign national prisoners, and 22.8 per cent of prisoners were from black and minority ethnic backgrounds.

The numbers and demographics were very different when the prison's life began. Wakefield's rich and unique history dates back all the way to the 1590s, when a House of Correction was established in the town, in what is now West Yorkshire. It was a place where prisoners, often awaiting either transportation or death, could be detained both before their trial and in the interval between trial and sentencing. For many years during its early history, the name Wakefield was virtually synonymous with going to prison.

Over time, several extensions to the House of Correction were built. With prisons increasingly used for punishment as well as a remand function, this broadened function and responsibility caused a spike in the prison population. An entirely new building was built in the 1840s. That building held responsibility for all prisoners over the West Riding until 1847, when Leeds Borough started to operate its own prison at Armley.

The historical, decentralised approach to the prison service waned during the 1800s, with central government control increasingly replacing the counties' control of prisons until it was formally abolished. Formalised in the Gaols Act of 1823, the justices were responsible for thorough prison inspections, and the Governor, Chaplain and Surgeon were expected to keep detailed daily diaries for reporting back to the courts of quarter sessions.

The justices' prison administration responsibility was still recognised in another act passed in 1835, but it was placed under Home Office regulations, and a national role profile for inspectors of prisons was established for consistency. Some scandals involving staff corruption and prison deaths created public support for increasingly central government control in the 1865 Prisons Act, and then total government control in the 1877 Prison Act. From the point of implementation of this act in April 1878, right through until 1963, the Home Secretary exercised control through prison commissioners.

At that point the commission was abolished, and its functions carried out directly by the Home Office. Of the 113 local prisons taken over, 38 were closed within five years, but Wakefield Prison not only survived this drastic cull, it was developed further. The registers indicate that most prisoners were serving quite short sentences for assault, petty theft or public drunkenness. A contract between the county justices and the War Office allowed military prisoners to be held at Wakefield until the 1870s (although as we shall see, war criminals were incarcerated there much more recently than that).

Civilian prisoners were transferred from the prison during the First World War, and it was repurposed as a military detention centre by the War Office from 1916 until it began to admit civilian inmates again in 1923. In the autumn of 1916, the closure of Dyce Work Camp meant that conscientious objectors were also sent to Wakefield. A group of them rebelled, went on strike and issued a set of demands for better treatment, the 'Wakefield Manifesto', in September 1918.

In terms of the age profile of prisoners, offenders under sixteen had been sent to reform school after an act was passed in 1854. At this point in its fascinating history, the female young offenders were at one reformatory and the boys were held at West Riding Reformatory School. The 1908 Prevention of Crime Act saw those aged sixteen to twenty-one sent to borstal rather than prison. The 1900s saw a reduction in short-stay prisoners.

***

Given its high security status, it is perhaps unsurprising that Wakefield was used to house IRA prisoners on and off. Whilst an attempt to break out IRA Chief of Staff Cathal Goulding in 1956 was aborted when the sirens sounded, as we shall describe later, the attempt to free Séamus Murphy in 1959 was successful, indeed the only successful recorded prison break from Wakefield. Frank Stagg died in Wakefield Prison on 12 February 1975 as part of a hunger strike by Provisional IRA prisoners. Our contributor Pete Wightman overlapped with a number of IRA prisoners in his long tenure at Wakefield and found it 'very demanding'.

'The staff were put through a lot of crap. The IRA made a hell of a lot of threats towards staff. You had to be really on your guard.'

The year 2001 saw the significant announcement that a new ultra-secure unit was to be built at Wakefield Prison, the first of its kind in the UK, and with the capability to house the most dangerous prisoners in Britain. Today, thanks in part to this new ultra-secure unit, Wakefield Prison is able to detain about 600 of Britain's most dangerous men – those on whole life sentences, murderers, paedophiles and rapists.

A highly critical inspection report was published in March 2004, written by Her Majesty's then-Chief Inspector of Prisons, Ann Owers. She noted, amongst many negatives, witnessing: 'One incident where a prisoner on crutches was handcuffed and the handcuffs jerked by the accompanying officer... We were concerned that prisoners in the [segregation] unit consistently referred to a climate of bullying and intimidation there. There were even a few allegations of assault.'

She went on to suggest that fear of reprisals was making prisoners reluctant to make formal complaints. The prison governor at the time, John Slater, vehemently denied the prisoner assault allegations. Owers said prisoners were reluctant to make formal complaints 'for fear of making things worse'.

Fascinatingly, the inspectors stated that Wakefield prisoners had their own phrase for the 'Disrespectful and even intimidatory behaviour of some officers, referred to as the Wakefield Way.'

All this amounted to what Owers memorably termed an 'atmosphere of disengagement amounting to disrespect'.

However, the more recent inspection reports, based on inspections conducted in 2018 and 2022, are far more positive. The most recent prison inspection of Wakefield, conducted late 2022 and published February 2023, was largely positive in its findings about the institution.

A key part of its summary noted:

This inspection of Wakefield is our first for four years, our last visit being in 2018 when we reported on a successful prison delivering some very good outcomes. Our findings at this inspection were similar, with outcomes assessed as reasonably good in three of our healthy prison tests: safety, respect, and rehabilitation. Only in purposeful activity did we find outcomes that were insufficient. While this represents some deterioration in purposeful activity and respect, in the context of the times and challenges faced by the prison system, this is one of the better inspections we have undertaken at an adult male prison recently.

The previous, 2018, inspection, though it is indeed largely positive as the latest report reiterates, did note the significant concern that there were unacceptable delays in getting those that needed psychiatric care transferred to a secure psychiatric hospital. This grabbed our attention given our work on Broadmoor, and we know all too well how crucial highly specialist care is to these individuals. The 2018 inspector, Peter Clarke, indicated that: 'Many prisoners across the prison estate are held in conditions that are not in any way therapeutic and indeed in many cases clearly exacerbate their condition.'

One particular 'exceptionally challenging to manage' individual stood out, who 'had complex needs that could not be met in the prison [and] his condition was deteriorating during a lengthy wait to be admitted to a secure hospital.'

***

The question of pastoral care around rehabilitation and mental health was one that we put to all our contributors. The advice of our staff contributor 'Jim' when handling prisoners was to treat them fairly and not to make promises that can't be kept. He remembered one particular prisoner.

Back in the mid-1970s, he had encountered a prisoner arrested for armed robbery. He was a difficult prisoner to handle. Jim then crossed paths with him again when he was serving a later sentence for murder – though the prisoner had assured Jim it had been 'just business'. As the prisoner remembered Jim as a firm but fair figure, the two discussed how their children were doing. A long-term relationship had been formed by that first impression many years before.

Jim has had a long, diverse and complex relationship with prison service work, which has provided him with a rich sense of Wakefield's recent past. Wakefield was the very first prison he visited when he joined the service decades ago. He worked there for four weeks as part of his training. He has also worked at another high-security prison which often swapped prisoners with Wakefield.

A 2017 Criminal Justice Inspectorate report had reviewed all the CSCs nationally, and described the CSC at Wakefield as providing: 'A secure and highly supervised environment for CSC prisoners who were unsuitable for other CSC units as a result of their behaviour'.

In other words, even in this highly specialised and exceptional of prisoner environments, Wakefield historically had a more hardcore version, and it continues to.

To return to his very personal connection with Wakefield's history, in 1992 Jim became responsible for policies around security and keeping good order at headquarters, and later oversaw the categorisation of category A prisoners.

Following the escapes of some IRA prisoners from another high-security institution, Jim helped to bring together high-security prisons and to reduce the risk of further escapes; he was the first director responsible for this and oversaw Wakefield when improving these security measures.

As part of his job, he would frequently visit high-security prisons on a regular monthly basis, to make sure that they were operating correctly. These prisons that he was, effectively, risk assessing on their security, included Wakefield.

Today, in his current senior prison service role, Jim remains partially responsible for the development of policies for handling difficult prisoners. As part of his role, he still visits Wakefield occasionally. When speaking about his biggest challenges when running a prison, Jim mused: 'Running a prison is a bit like plate spinning.'

He elaborated that, whilst some issues are easier to manage than others, not one is more important than the other. Ultimately, they all require attention to stay afloat. The difficulty arises when having to manage everything at once, not concentrating on specifics but on the whole picture. In this high-pressure scenario, you are constantly checking to get an advance warning if something is going wrong and you deal with it before it becomes a problem.

Another reason for this is to avoid aggrieved prisoners; treating prisoners as they should be treated and keeping to a schedule avoids the potential of prisoners banding together to protest, which can lead to a much larger issue. Here, we had some good insights from Hayley Grocock, who is Chief Executive Officer of Wakefield District Sight Aid. She strongly reiterated this point in the context of her knowledge of the prisoners' Braille work, and its therapeutic qualities. We will look at her work in greater detail later in the book.

Jim noted that in his experience, the appeal of prison work has notably decreased over the years; in the modern day, staff turnover at prisons such as Wakefield is a lot higher. Part of this is due to the pay not being as competitive, but also that the prison service is attracting much younger staff into an environment with a smaller progression scale than before. Because of this limited progression and less competitive pay, a lot more people are leaving after a few years, whereas in the past people would often stay for decades at a time.

The appeal of the job for Jim was the challenge of helping people to manage and survive their imprisonment. He was fascinated by 'the degree of conflict and cooperation' involved in the job to keep a prison 'stable, decent and secure'. He also noted that a career in prison service was often a strategic one, and he thrived in what he called 'a very long-term world', wherein prisoners would remember their interactions with you for years, and the ability to interact with them years after your first encounter with them would depend on how you treated them in that first instance.

In support of Jim's points about the need to show decency as well as stability and security, over the years Wakefield has 'played host' to many individuals who are not necessarily the usual suspects. Not every inmate of Monster Mansion was a monster by today's standards. Fred Haslam was incarcerated there for being a conscientious objector in the First World War. Klaus Fuchs, sentenced to fourteen years in British prisons for supplying British and American nuclear weapon research to Russia (then the USSR), served part of his term at Wakefield, from 1951 to 1959. Stefan Ivan Kiszko, wrongly convicted of murder, served time there, too.

One inmate offered us their fascinating view of the recent history of the institution.

Some history about HMP W. They have a famous tree there, it is called the Mulberry tree. As the song says, here we go round the mulberry tree the mulberry tree. This, so I am told, goes back years when prisoners were exercised and had to walk around that tree. The area where the tree is, is no longer in use for exercise. The clock tower is still there and still works. On C wing at the bottom, the last two cells were actually used for the death sentence by hanging. The two cells and the two basement cells directly underneath were also used as the drop down from the gallows. This is fact. When the death penalty was abolished, a floor was put in, the outer brick walls were rebuilt due to the construction on the floors [removing the gallows]. From outside C wing, to this very day you can actually still see the change in the bricks from where in the 1960s it was rebuilt.

Staff changes in the last five years: HMP W, with other prisons, changed the age for retirement. This in an endeavour to force the officers to work for more years. However, the old school staff, all the experienced staff were under the old contract. They was given the chance to retire or stay on part time and finish when they wanted to. Had they chosen to stay full time then they was asked to sign up to the new contracts of employment. Having spoken to staff about this it was clear they all decided to go part time. Indeed, as they have said, by going part time and now receiving their pension, with the part-time income combined with their pension they were working less hours now and receiving the same money as they did when full time. As a result of this, a lot of good experienced staff were lost. Over the past five years the prison service have gone on a recruitment exercise. Many of the staff now working in the prison service are quite inexperienced, which has potential implications for the safety standards in prisons.

***

Our contributor Vanessa Frake-Harris, a retired Prison Governor, has sharp eyes, spiky hair and a stylish grey pair of glasses. She is a warm, intelligent, focused and humane woman, who gave us so much food for thought and insight during our research for this book. Amongst many other topics, we were interested in Vanessa's take on some of the unique historical features at Wakefield, which is a truly historic site, not always for all the wrong reasons.

How did Vanessa come to have a connection with Wakefield at all? She had been working at HMP Holloway – the largest women's prison in western Europe until it closed its doors in 2016 – in north London as a senior officer and looking to transfer.

A friend's father was working at Wakefield, and he offered to show Vanessa around. She went up there and had a look. We were particularly interested in her first impressions from the perspective of someone who knew other notorious prisons intimately, including Holloway and Wormwood Scrubs.

She described it as 'not a huge prison', especially when

compared to Scrubs. 'It's a very old Victorian jail, as is Scrubs, but it was all single cell, it was a radial prison. To me, it reminded me of what an actual prison should look like, a proper radial prison, so a centre in the middle and you've got the spurs going off.'

What was there that distinguished it from any other jail she had worked at or been into?

What struck me the most was at bang up [bang up is prison slang for locking a prisoner up in their cell] there is a – or there used to be – a huge great big bell in the centre. And somebody rang the bell. And literally the whole jail stopped, prisoners went to their cells, and they stood in the doorway of their cell waiting to be locked behind their door. Now, having worked at Scrubs, I can assure you, I spent hours and hours chasing prisoners. 'Oh miss, just gotta get this', 'Oh gov, can I just give this to my mate', totally chasing them round the wing, trying to get them behind the doors. But the regime at Wakefield was very different, almost austere.

The bell that she recalls is a notably interesting historic feature of Wakefield, which several of our other contributors also remarked upon.

In a report by the Chief Inspector of Prisons (HMCIP), it noted that there is a very fine line between security and decency for a healthy prison. In order to maintain control, you have to balance the two, and Wakefield had strayed into the very secure jail area. Although this was very appropriate for somewhere with such an ultra-category A status, perhaps inevitably it led to the detriment of some other practical parts of daily life, like schedules and classes for prisoners. It is a very fine line and you want to stay directly in the middle of it.

For all the distinctions and differences that struck Vanessa, ultimately there were many generic features and similarities too. 'The atmosphere was a typical jail, to be honest. It was very routine-driven. Staff knew what they were doing, prisoners knew what they were doing, and it all seemed to flow very nicely.'

She even went so far as to say that a part of her wishes that she had made the decision to transfer there, but she was a southern girl, her life was based in the south, and she just was not ready to move up north and make such a permanent change. As she explained, it is a lot to uproot your whole life, and she didn't know anyone in the vicinity of Wakefield.

She also looked at Frankland, which was 'even further up'. HMP Frankland is in Brasside, Durham, and rather like the Wakefield/New Hall arrangement, it is situated very near a 'sister' prison, the notorious closed women's prison HMP Low Newton.

Vanessa has a soft spot for old Victorian jails as they have such character and history, perhaps none more so than Wakefield. 'As long as they provide decency, security and a good regime, then I'm all for keeping them. They should only really be considered for closure if one of those three pillars begins to slip.'

For a category A like Wakefield, although everybody we met indicated a genuine commitment to those three pillars of decency, security and a good regime, albeit with varying degrees of success, security is arguably always going to come first. We were keen to explore what even makes a category A a category A in the first place?

Chapter 2

The Prison System

A s someone who was directly responsible for overseeing the categorisation of category A prisoners, our contributor Jim was asked what factors would dictate such a decision. He explained that he would have to ask himself: 'If they were free, at that time, would they present a severe risk to members of the public or to the security of the state or the police or those who would have to deal with them? You're trying to pick out the people who, if they were free, would be really dangerous.'

The UK has eight maximum security prisons for adult males, which between them hold the vast majority of Britain's most ill-famed prisoners, as well as those serving life sentences. In addition to HMP Wakefield, they are Frankland, Full Sutton, Long Lartin, Belmarsh, Manchester, Whitemoor and Woodhill. Many of the prisoners described in this book move between these prisons during their sentences, such as Levi Bellfield and Charles Bronson.

As a prisoner succinctly described to us:

HMP Wakefield is a part of the HSE [High Security Estate]. Other prisons within the estate are, Long Lartin, Full Sutton, Frankland, Belmarsh, Manchester and Whitemoor. High Security holds category A and high-risk offenders. In short, the conditions must be so that it is impossible to escape. For triple category A prisoners they would be held on the HSU [high security unit] at HMP Belmarsh. This is the only HSU in the UK. This I have been located on in the past. It is a prison within a prison. It has its own reception area and also has a tunnel which leads direct to Woolwich Crown Court. Therefore, one can walk from the prison directly into the court room. HMP Wakefield does not have a VP [vulnerable persons] status. This is actually bizarre when you consider other prisons all have VP units. VP units, as they are called, house child sex offenders, child murderers, rapists, and those who have committed heinous acts and are a target of attack by other mainstream prisoners such as armed robbers, hitmen and organised crime.

To take a step back, the eight notorious high-security prisons are all within the UK Prison Service. His Majesty's Prison Service is responsible for the management of prisons in England and Wales, as well as serving as the National Offender Management Service for England and Wales.

The Northern Ireland Prison Service and the Scottish Prison Service manage those two countries respectively. The three Crown Dependencies, the Isle of Man and the Bailiwicks of Jersey and Guernsey (the Channel Islands), also have their own separate services.

Across the United Kingdom, there are four categories of security for all male adult prisoners. There are different designations, as we will explain, for women and young offenders.

Fundamentally, the categories for male prisoners are based on their crime, sentence, the risk of escape and violent tendencies. The latter combines a risk assessment of both internal and external threat. What risk do they pose to the control and stability of a prison, and what is the likelihood of them harming the public if they escape? Every male prisoner over the age of eighteen is given a security categorisation soon after they enter prison.

Designated with the letters A to D, category A is the highest level of security (and Wakefield is very much in that category), and category D is the lowest level of security. Category A, B and C prisons are known as closed prisons, while category D prisons are called open prisons.

So, for male prisons in the United Kingdom:

Category A are high-security prisons, housing men who pose the highest threat to national security, the police, and/or the public if they were to escape. Amongst the offences that can land men in a category A are plenty that you would expect: murder or attempted murder, rape or attempted rape, sexual assault, manslaughter, wounding with intent, kidnapping and terrorism offences. However, men have also been banged up for offences under the Official Secrets Act, possessing or supplying explosives, armed robbery and importing or supplying class A controlled substances.

We discovered when we were writing our first book about the 2015 Hatton Garden heist how shocked and distressed prisoners were to be banged up on remand in the category A jail HMP Belmarsh with all the murderers, when all they had done was steal from a vault.

Belmarsh does seem to have a particularly odd mixture of criminals, with some of the most horrifying killers of recent times, including Stephen Port, the 'Grindr killer', Wayne Couzens (now at Frankland) and Ian Huntley, but also Julian Assange and previously the Great Train Robber Ronnie Biggs, Jonathan Aitken and Jeffrey Archer.

Unsurprisingly, an awful lot of scrutiny is put on the risk of prisoners in category A escaping. As part of this, category A prisoners get split into Standard Risk, High Risk and Exceptional Risk on the basis of their likelihood of escaping. There is also a Provisional category A condition. That's for men who are waiting to be tried on the most serious of offences, and therefore cannot be held in category B conditions like the vast majority of men on remand.

There's a special list for those naughty cons who have actively tried to escape. They are put on their holding prison's Escape List. We have sometimes heard them called E List Men or E Men. They have to be cuffed and to wear bright clothing that stands out from the crowd when they are being moved inside and outside the prison. They also get moved frequently from one cell to another and have some of their clothing and personal effects confiscated from their cell before they are locked in at night. This is all intended to prevent an escape.

Category B prisons are local or training prisons. Training prisons hold long-term and high-security prisoners, and local prisons hold prisoners that are taken from court in the local area, whether on remand or after sentencing. Men in this category are not deemed to require maximum security, but it's still seen as very important to make sure that they don't escape.

Category C prisons are training and resettlement prisons. They house the majority of male prisoners in the UK. With a focus on reskilling and rehabilitation, they are there to maximise prisoners' chances of effectively reintegrating back into society when they get out. These men can't be trusted in open conditions yet, but they are not likely to try and escape either.

Category D are open prisons, with minimal security, because it seems reasonable to assume that they won't abuse the privilege and escape. Prisoners in category D prisons are allowed out for most of the day on licence for education and work. Prisoners don't get into a category D unless they have been risk-assessed and deemed suitable for open conditions, so not many Wakefield prisoners have a chance of ending up in one any time soon. These prisons are commonly known as 'D Cat'. The licence to work or learn in the community is known as ROTL: Release on Temporary Licence. Normally about a quarter of a way through their sentence, these prisoners can also go on home leave once they have passed their FLED: Full Licence Eligibility Date.

* * *

Our contributor Jim compared the categorisation of dangerous prisoners with the memorable analogy of working in a chemical lab. Spilling some non-dangerous chemicals would be 'no worse than spilling water, versus something that if it spilled, it would corrosively burn its way through anything it hit. So you really take care with the more corrosive liquid.'

Much in the same way, dangerous prisoners should be guarded by higher security measures to further prevent risk of escape or harm to other individuals.

Jim noted that this categorisation can change over time, depending if someone is no longer considered a risk. An obvious example of this, and not uncommon with the lifers at Wakefield, could be a prisoner who has reduced mobility or is much older than when he was first categorised. Naturally, these are factors that make them less of a threat; however, other factors are also taken into consideration. Prisoners are constantly under assessment, being regularly seen by psychologists and the probationary, and prisoner responses to these being taken into account.

Another contributing factor is whether the prisoner is actively pursuing the same behaviours that would have led to their imprisonment. Jim listed two potential examples of such behaviours: a paedophile who was trying to get hold of pictures of children, and a drug addict keeping in touch with associates, smuggling or taking drugs. As just one instance, we see the example later in Chapter 9 of Ian Watkins apparently using a contraband mobile phone to try and groom a young female on the outside.

Jim noted that there was a key balance in these observations. That balance is to be realistic but not too pessimistic. People are capable of change; if every category A prisoner perpetually remained in that category, the system would be overwhelmed.

However, he did mention that he had observed several people engaging in a long-term attempt to present differently in order to be re-categorised into a lower security category. He recalled a prisoner who had been arrested due to his work as a gang leader. He had been an intelligent man, and also happened to be a fine artist; the prisoner attempted to present that because of his skills with art that he had changed and therefore 'didn't need any security'. However, his time in prison had revealed him to be a manipulative and organised character. Consequently, he was not re-categorised. As expected, upon the completion of his sentence and after his release, he reoffended and was imprisoned due to his continued work as a gang leader. This time it was linked to class A drug importations. It is recidivists such as this that make the judgement calls of the parole board extremely tricky. Jim went on to explain that as well as prisoner categorisation, there are other means to increase prisoner security, particularly for problematic or unpredictable individuals who are deemed too dangerous to be around normal prisoners. These prisoners are placed in smaller units with specialised 'therapeutic interventions' in order to help to manage them; the aim is to keep these numbers as small as possible, with the eventual goal of returning them to normal wing successfully. He notes that whilst these types of interventions he specifically mentions are not part of Wakefield, he has experience of them at other high-security prisons such as Frankland.

Most prisoners who utilise these units are what would be described as 'personality disordered', wherein people are 'wired differently' and behave oddly but are not necessarily associated with any kind of mental disorder. Jim noted that at the beginning of his career this often included people with autism, which at that time was harder to diagnose, though now we have a much deeper understanding of such conditions. Although there is still much further to go, autism is not demonised in the same way as it would have been prior to this greater understanding – we have a lot to thank medical and psychological advancements for in this aspect. Within these 'therapeutic intervention' units, different specialists, psychologists and nurses would work together as a team to help the individual with a tailored approach, making it clear that 'this is a place in which you can change'.

Jim recalled to us visiting another prison in 2009 to

2010. There, he met with prisoners within these units, many of whom he recognised from previous interactions as difficult prisoners. He observed that the prisoners were much more relaxed than previously and seemed very appreciative of the world. Jim describes having had thoughtful, reflective conversations with them that would have been very difficult to have had previously, something he regards as a high achievement. Jim concludes that whilst significant, positive change is possible, the desire to reform must come from within; the prisoner has to have a genuine desire to change for the better.

'They've got to change, you can't change them. If they don't want to change, there's nobody who can sort of wave a magic wand and change somebody.'

Jim noted that the prisoners receiving these specialised therapeutic interventions would not be segregated from other prisoners, but would be contained together on a separate wing; indeed, it's discouraged to keep prisoners in long-term segregation from other people.

Jim noted that Wakefield does have two or three prisoners who are kept in total, long-term segregation, and live in specialised cells to accommodate this long-term living arrangement, though he emphasised that this number of prisoners is extremely low.

As Paul Powell, a former SO and PO, told us, in terms of the segregation unit schedule: 'Prisoners were unlocked and went down for their meals one at a time rather than all together, because they were segregated from other prisoners, so they'd never meet. They did exercise together though, but that was the only time they were allowed to be together.'

Fascinatingly, the segregation unit was his favourite area: 'There's not one area I can say I didn't enjoy working in.' He enjoyed the segregation unit as an SO because 'it was so busy and so challenging, and the staff we had were excellent and we were a really good team.'

We know from our research that the segregation unit at Wakefield can house up to six prisoners, but this is such an extreme solution that not all of the segregation cells are necessarily occupied. It was particularly lively when it was Robert Maudsley and Charlie Bronson in there together, as we shall come to later.

It's usually different for women and young people. In really exceptional circumstances women and young adults can be held in a category A prison, but normally if they are deemed high risk, they are categorised as 'restricted status', which means that they can only be held in a closed prison. As with men, they are held in either closed or open confinement based on the risk they present and their needs as an inmate. Like men, women are split into four categories. They are:

Restricted Status, which is similar to category A for male prisoners.

Closed is similar to category B for men: these women are not deemed to require Restricted Status but escape still has to be made almost impossible for them.

Semi-open lasted for a bit as a female category at the beginning of the millennium. Introduced in 2001, it was intended for those who were unlikely to escape but could not yet be trusted in an open prison. It was phased out pretty quickly, though, and the women's prisons HMP Drake Hall and HMP Morton Hall were re-designated as closed in March 2009.

Open is for those who can reasonably be trusted not to escape.

As with men, female remand prisoners in the UK are always held in closed prisons.

John Hartshorne, now a Consultant after a long career in the prison service, was able to bring these categories to life for us quite a bit. He explained to us that:

Whilst male prisons such as Wakefield are categorised by letters: A, B, C and D, female prisons are separated into two categories: Open and Closed. Open female prisons are for the equivalent of D category prisoners, with closed prisons equivalent to A, B and C prisoners, so there is more diversity of types of prisoners under one roof. Category A equivalent female prisoners are referred to as 'restricted status prisoners', who are kept under the same strict protocols as male category A. Female prisons also have a mother and baby unit, so prisoners who are pregnant can give birth in prison; mothers who cannot be separated from their children can in fact raise them from inside prison walls.

It is very difficult to imagine compounding what is already one of life's most stressful experiences – childbirth – by adding a custodial sentence into the mix. It's hard not to feel a pang of sympathy for any woman in that situation, whatever her crime, as long as it was not cruelty towards children.

For younger offenders, YOIs, Young Offender Institutions, house prisoners aged between eighteen and twenty-one. Youth Custody is for people under eighteen who are either on remand or have already been sentenced to a period of detention by the courts.

It seems pretty clear that there is an art as well as a science to all of this, and, as something that is rigorous but also judgement-based, mistakes can be made.

It's also a system of categorisation and it's only fair and sensible that it undergoes review by prison staff, not just when prisoners are sentenced but throughout their time in prison. If their risk is assessed to go up or down, then prison staff can action a transfer to a more suitable category of prison. This means that a prisoner does not necessarily stay in the same category throughout their sentence.

A re-categorisation can happen at any time, to either sentenced or convicted prisoners, if something happens or new information comes out that has a real impact on their risk assessment.

Outside of these exceptional circumstances, if a prisoner is sentenced to over four years in prison, they are assessed annually until the last two years of their sentence, when their assessment steps up to every six months. If they are sentenced to between one and four years – which tends not to apply to Wakefield inmates – they are assessed every six months. Wakefield and all category A prisons require prison staff to work with the Prison Service head office to check security. In a category D prison, there is no need for prisoners to have a change of category unless their risks have changed.

Of course, plenty of prisoners are not happy with their category or their re-categorisation. What happens then? They can appeal against it. This has to be done by filing a complaint through the prison complaint system that each individual prison is responsible for. First, they might flag their grievance with their key worker. That key worker can relay the unhappiness to the prisoner's POM – Prison Offender Manager – who can give them more context about the decision. If that isn't satisfactory, the complaint can be escalated through the normal procedure. The prison staff have to provide the reasons behind their decision. If a review ends up taking place, it should be done by someone senior to the original decision-maker. The prison needs to give the prisoner a written copy of the categorisation decision and the reasons why that decision was made. This information is then used by the prisoner when they write their appeal.

* * *

Michael Sams is a recent, and highly notorious, Wakefield inmate who appealed for a re-categorisation. Back in

March 2012, he made a bid to re-categorise down from category A, arguing to the High Court judge that he was less of a danger to women prison staff than he had been. His appeal was rejected. Much more recently, he had a parole denial in April 2023. The panel were reviewing a few different possibilities, including whether he could be transferred to an open prison and whether he was suitable for release.

His probation officer had put together a release plan, with part of it indicating specifically that he would 'reside in designated accommodation for an extended period of time as well as [have] strict limitations on [his] contacts, movements and activities', however 'the panel concluded this plan was not robust enough to manage Mr Sams in the community.' He was not seen as meeting the criteria for a transfer to an open prison either. On that point, the panel has to look at issues such as the nature of his offence, any progress towards rehabilitation he had made during his many years in Wakefield, and other evidence. Sams did not give evidence himself, but he was at the hearing.

In July 1991, Michael Sams, born 11 August 1941, kidnapped Julie Dart, a sex worker just eighteen years of age, and subsequently murdered her after she tried to escape. In January 1992, having not been caught for the appalling killing of young Julie, he kidnapped estate agent Stephanie Slater and raped her during her terrible ordeal. He released her after a ransom was paid. As the panel were no doubt weighing up, Sams very much remained a danger to women once he had been convicted and imprisoned. In

Wakefield in October 1995, he attacked a female probation officer with a metal spike. This horrible attack went to trial at Durham Crown Court in February 1997, and he was handed an additional eight years on what was already a life sentence for his crime.

Because he was an SO at the time, we wanted to ask Pete about Michael Sams. Pete was an SO at the time [the ranking goes officer, SO, PO, Chief then Governor]. Pete smiled grimly as he remembered.

He complained about everything. Anything and everything. He was right into railways, as you can imagine: that's where he did most of his crimes. He had loads of railway books, but they were only allowed so many books in possession and he was forever putting apps in to exchange books in reception or people to bring property in. He was always complaining about the state of the beds. I remember one particular funny time. He came to the office to complain about his mattress.

Pete was writing something down. At that time, they had cleaning officers on the wings who took care of the cleaners, and did all the general duties. One of the cleaning officers was sitting next to him.

Picture the scene, Michael Sams, he's at the window on his one leg, complaining about the state of the mattress and how he couldn't sleep and it were unfair and inhumane and all these things against what he had done to his poor victims. So this cleaning officer said, 'Listen kid, you wanna try sleeping in a fucking wheelie bin.' And Christ Almighty I nearly choked on my coffee. He just stared at him and walked off.

Pete also was there when Sams tried to take the Vicar's wife hostage.

All the visitors were told when they came onto a wing to report to the wing office, and report to staff that they were on the wing and for what purpose. She used to come on the threes landing: firsts were at the bottom, twos was normal wing where you first come in, and threes and fours were at the top. She would enter from the chaplaincy and walk onto the threes or onto the fours and not tell the staff that she were on the wing. Obviously, Michael Sams were watching her do this. She came on one particular day, and he dragged her into an office to take her hostage. He would have seriously hurt her had it not been for another prisoner. It were a prisoner who saved her. He went in and smacked him. He risked his life. That's the type of people that we worked with.

Pete went on:

That's the reason there were such strict rules in place about alerting staff of your presence, to ensure staff are not put at risk, and she didn't listen. You always told fellow officers where you were going. If I went to the toilet I'd say to my staff, 'I'm just nipping to the loo.' If I were going off the wing I'd say, 'Just nipping to Admin, I'm just nipping to centre,' so everybody knew where everybody was. She never came in the jail again. She was only kept hostage for a matter of minutes. She was dragged in, a prisoner saw and immediately went in after her and saved her. Never gave him time to establish himself.

Sams was taken down to the seg.

He weren't allowed his false leg in the segregation unit, so he had to hop around everywhere which were rather funny to watch. Going to the servery, you could only go to the servery once, as they were let out one at a time to go and get their food. At that time, they were served soup, main course, pudding (or duff as it was called) and a pot of tea. So he had to try and carry everything hopping. Well that just doesn't work. And the staff wouldn't carry anything for him, because he was such a vile horrible sod, the staff wouldn't do anything that they didn't have to do for him.

In terms of legitimate candidacy for re-categorisation, Sams would seem to be pretty low down the list. On the basis of his age and these failed appeals, Sams is highly likely to die behind bars in Wakefield.

Chapter 3

Prison Life

What happens, though, if the upshot of that categorisation, as with Sams and our prisoner contacts, lands you in Wakefield? What's it really like in there? We wanted to know from the prisoner and the staff perspective too.

Before we get into all the details, we want to share an intriguing insight into Wakefield that a prisoner offered us about what happens in practice after all that complex categorisation of prisoners we have just described. Even within a category A, after all, there is a pretty broad church in terms of both the crimes committed and, particularly, the ongoing danger that they might present.

HMP W and the mixing of prisoners – non VPs [vulnerable prisoners] and VPs. This is very odd as not many prisons do this. In prisons like Frankland, Full Sutton, Long Lartin, mainstream prisoners [not VPs] are kept separate at all times because given the chance they would attack a VP. Take my landing, the threes, at HMP W. The row I was on. There was a baby killer, Andrew Lloyd from Swansea, Wales. Next door to him was a Black Yardie, Betee Gordon from London. He and his brother were in jail for a shooting [murder] in London. Next to Gordon was Ronald Castree, a child rapist and child killer [high profile]. Then Mick Baxter, an armed robber from Leeds, and so it went on. These people were actually living next door to each other there. So how did it work? The mainstream inmates would simply refuse to acknowledge and speak to the VPs. They never mixed with them. Nonces would mix with each other, rapists with each other and mainstreams with each other. Many mainstreams who arrived at HMP W would spend months in the segregation unit refusing to locate because of the monsters who were held there. After months of isolation, they would eventually concede and locate. A message would get back to them, just locate and mix with the mainstreams only. Indeed, the mainstreams would take money off the nonces.

An old saying, 'A nonce's money is as good as anyone else's.' They would lower their rules if they were being paid protection money. Ian Watkins is an example of this, a bad nonce, but the person who lent him the phone, and eventually charged him £5,000 for losing the phone was a Liverpool gangster who was a high-risk category A prisoner who was in jail for throwing grenades at a rival drug gang and shootings. Even though they took

*money off nonces the fact remains… if a mainstream
wants a move out the jail they will attack a VP simply
to facilitate a move.*

*You have to consider the public interest in prosecuting
them for the assault. The average sentence is life with
a high tariff, twenty to forty years minimum to serve.
A prisoner serving life with a minimum of thirty years
has nothing to lose. For an assault of a beating or
minor slashing, the CPS [Crown Prosecution Service]
might not prosecute because the sentence that could be
imposed would only run current with the thirty years
they are serving. If the prisoner went not guilty (which
they would) it would cost the public purse thousands of
pounds to run a trial. Therefore such incidents are dealt
with through the prison punishment policy. Segregation
and loss of wages.*

Our contributor Lisa Powell, now retired from Wakefield,
though, unlike the prisoner, could see the rationale behind
both sex offenders wanting to keep quiet, and prisoners in
for other offences mixing: 'Nobody wants trouble, nobody
wants any bother. It's very strange. They kind of put
blinkers on and get on with whatever's there.'

Not wanting trouble and not getting trouble are two
very different things at Wakefield though. One prisoner,
who has done time in several different prisons, believes
in his opinion there are things about the structure of
Wakefield that could affect its safety.

1. *Staff simply sit at the end of each landing. Normally two or three staff.*

2. *The influx of new underexperienced young, vulnerable staff being employed due to many leaving the prison service.*

3. *HMP W has some blind spots, by example the huge centre stairwell makes viewing from one end to the other virtually impossible. I remind you of the attack on Wayne Gasgoin. He lay there for nearly half an hour unconscious before staff noticed him.*

4. *The exercise yard – most prisons now have an exercise yard for each wing. However, HMP W has one yard for four wings. At HMP W, all the wings share the yard at the same time. With this comes gangs all meeting up from different wings, with gangs from other wings all meeting up comes bigger numbers of each gang.*

5. *The moves to employment are all done at once. Most other prisons will restrict the movements to each wing at a time, to reduce the numbers moving and clashing with other wing movements.*

Violence in prisons can never be stopped, as stated many have nothing to lose given their long sentences. However, surely prevention should be in place. The last point on safety at HMP W is this: it holds VP prisoners and non-VP prisoners together. Like oil and water, it will never mix!'

Jo Taylor's first day at Wakefield was quite a baptism of fire. A Cat A had got on the roof of a building. Following this incident, the rules changed so that Cat A prisoners couldn't go through areas leading to it.

Jo noted some very interesting and unexpected contrasts between Wakefield and New Hall in her first impressions. 'At New Hall they shout out of their cells. Wakefield is very quiet. The floor was wet because they had polished it. It is a lot cleaner at Wakefield than the women's prison.' Wakefield was her first time in a men's prison. Jo did ten years at New Hall and five years at Wakefield.

> *I thought the men were monsters. I didn't fear the women, even though women would attack. Before I joined Wakefield, someone had taken a prison officer hostage. She was trapped for over twenty-four hours. 'Shoot the bolts' means unlock the cell door so they can never close you in because the bolt has come out. They didn't do shoot the bolt at Wakefield. I couldn't believe they didn't do it.*

When Jo interrogated this, the response was 'Oh, they like to be able to close their own cell door!' Jo explained:

> *I was on C wing and then on A wing. Similar looking (google it). D wing was a horrible wing. C and A wing had big wide staircases… The wings go off on… you saw a clocktower when you look out the window. It's like you've cut your pie in half, and the half has four slices:*

A, B, C, D wing, hospital unit and seg... There was a mixture of prisoners on all of them nonces, serial killers, murderers, terrorists. In the seg: Bronson, Maudsley and Shipman was there. Maudsley has a cell door with a gate.

Monster Mansion's accommodation comprises, as Jo explained, all single-occupancy cells with built-in sanitation.

Nobody shares a cell at Wakefield, there are no doubles. All the cells are the same size. Toilet, sink, bed, quilt, TV, they can buy things to make it more [home-like]. Most prisoners come in with nothing... some clothes. You can't change the fabric of the cell. They've got a noticeboard, they can put pictures up. Anything they decorate with will just come off. There's just a toilet in the cell. A little table, maybe a cupboard. New Hall has some doubles with bunk beds. I think they do have a curtain for the toilet... You've got to have a way with cons and you develop that after time.

Jo went on to say of the single cells in Wakefield: 'They've got the life of Riley, really.' She described to us three different tiers of prison privileges at Wakefield: Enhanced, Standard and Basic. These different standards are determined by the inmates' behaviour in prison, not their crimes.

One prisoner gave us a very comprehensive description of the wings at Wakefield.

HMP W has four main wings. The four wings interlock to a main centre.

Each wing holds 180 offenders. At the end of each there are barred gates, therefore one cannot openly walk onto another wing. The prison is Victorian and very old, and indeed falling apart in places. There are four very long landings on each wing, in prison terms offenders call each landing the ones, twos, threes and fours. The landings are not open plan; each side is lined with cells with very thin walkways. The cells are painted brick with little windows that do not open fully. There is a cage on the outside to prevent what offenders call 'A Line' being passed. This is when you rip up a bed sheet and place a kit bag on the end and swing it to another cell when you are in lock down. The windows in any event only open about two inches max.

When you walk onto a wing you are walking directly onto the twos landing. The very first part of the landing is open plan. There is a small staff observation office on the left of each wing, on the right-hand side there is a closed office with just a door entrance. This is where the senior officer and custody managers offices are located. There is a huge centre stairwell that takes you up to the threes and fours landings. The ones landing is effectively in the basement. The set-up is identical on every wing.

So to the cells... people believe HMP W, or prisons in general, are luxurious. This is certainly misleading. There is a sink, a toilet, a bed and some cheap fixed wall lockers to hold your personal effects. Being a high-

security prison, the prison service are aware of all the hiding places. so make it very difficult to conceal items. The sink is stainless steel, with it housed in a stainless steel case from the floor upwards. It is completely sealed in. It is held together with rivets not screws as these can be undone by offenders using nail clippers and tweezers, which offenders will use and make screwdrivers from. They can be shaped by scraping against the wall. The toilets at HMP W are also stainless steel with no toilet seat. These too are also sealed in with stainless steel. Stainless steel holds the smell of urine, the metal absorbs it and no matter how much you clean it the smell never goes, within the summer months it can be unbearable. The beds are all steel tubes sealed into one unit and bolted to the floor. The base is steel straps all welded together. The mattress is made from anti-fire black foam and covered with a sealed heavy-duty blue rubber-type plastic. The pillows are the same.

The sheets are thin green cotton, the blankets are woollen, itchy, orange and dark green in colour. There is a small picture board attached to the wall for offenders to put photos of family on if they so choose. The flooring is concrete with a permanent attached hard lino. The walls are all painted the same throughout, magnolia. You are given a strip of double-sided tape for the thin cotton curtains. The televisions are small in size and nothing like the TVs in society, again security is in play, therefore all the cases are see-through plastic and sealed, i.e. you can see all the wires.

Everything within the TV is visible. The doors are old steel doors and notwithstanding the reinforced lock on the door, there are also two bolts on the outside of the door, one at the top, one at the bottom of the door, which are used every night. The size of the cells are 10 feet in length and 6 feet in width. Not very spacious at all, you are on top of everything.

The wings are known as A, B, C and D wings. Staff will have a table at the end of each wing landing and sit and observe the offenders. The tables are situated at one end of the landings only. While security is tight re. contraband, the safety of offenders is very poor. The length of the landings are the length of a football pitch. With staff sitting at one end of the landing it would be difficult to observe anyone getting attacked at the other end of the landing or in a cell. I have been involved in serious assaults there and witnessed many, of which I will come to later.'

Jo had told us: 'There is a spending limit in Wakefield but on Enhanced [tier] you could spend more money. They could book their own food. They could make cakes, pizzas, curries, you could get everything from a canteen list.'

As Jo explained, all of the residential units have their own kitchens where well-behaved inmates can prepare their own food.

A prisoner described the cooking facilities to us, too.

On each wing is a small kitchen area to allow prisoners to cook, there are no nice big cookers, just two standard electric cookers with four rings and an oven. HMP W has a high Muslim population and fights are often a regular thing because they try to take over the cookers and claim they should be halal. To resolve this the cookers are self-policed by the inmates, the Muslims use one cooker, the non-Muslims use the other cooker. However, fights often happen over bacon spitting onto the other cooker. It is never ending there.

The exercise yard is a little small yard with grass in the centre and a concrete circle going around in a circle shape. Staff will not actually come onto the exercise yard area in fear of being attacked. There is 12-foot fence with razor wire on the top and prisoners are locked in the huge cage. There is a huge gang culture there and the yard is similar to a USA type scenario. You enter the yard at a set time of the day – it can be in the morning prior to work, then come out and go to work, or coming back from work. As you walk on the yard there are places where the gangs will all stand together. On the right-hand side as you walk in the cage all the Muslims will stand together. To the left about 30 feet away all the blacks will stand together, at the far bottom all the foreign nationals will stand together. The people smugglers and organised crime lot. The nobodies will just walk around the concrete path with their own friends.

There is a Braille shop at Wakefield where offenders convert books into Braille. Our wonderful contributor Hayley has been involved in this activity and finds it very rewarding, as an intellectual stimulation for the prisoners as well as good for the wider community. We will go into more details about its rehabilitative powers from Hayley's perspective later in the book.

This is not the only work she was aware of the men doing; they also get the chance to do furniture restoration for charity. 'The men fix and upcycle second-hand furniture and it gets fixed and sold to furniture shops to raise money for the local hospice. It's extraordinary. If it had a label saying "made by the men of Wakefield Prison", would people like it or not? It could go either way. There must be mental health benefits in all kinds of ways though. The process itself is quite healing for people.'

Vanessa mentioned that the company Timpson come into Wakefield quite often to teach classes and train prisoners.

However, Timpson do a lot of work with prisoners and employ ex-prisoners, as well. Things that help prisoners to have a responsibility, have a trade, something to apply to the real world.

Timpson are also involved with prisoners at New Hall. Michelle was the instructional officer for the Timpson Foundation whilst working at New Hall prison. Timpson has an academy there which is set up just like a Timpson shop. Women can come for workshops, learn everything about working at Timpson with the hope of a job upon release. James Timpson has a long history of good work employing ex-offenders and giving them a second chance. For Michelle, 'You quickly realised they're just like everybody else. It's just a normal person coming to work.'

The people that run the academies have to be vetted and do prison training before going in. Personal protection, key safety, radio training. There are also personal alarms in the workshops in case anything should go wrong, but in the eight years she worked in New Hall Michelle never had to use any of these alarms or protection measures. She always took the additional precaution of 'take yourself in and nothing else!'

The scheme is a game-changer for prisoners, some of whom have never worked before. It gives them experience of what it's like to work in the real world and prepares them for release. The work might involve introducing them to computer systems. When they begin work at a Timpson branch, they already know what they're doing and it's not 'another hurdle for them to get over'.

The workshop can involve group sessions or sometimes one-to-one assessments and training. If something goes missing they have to report it and then it's handed over to the security team to deal with. Michelle never had anybody refuse to work, and found that people in the academy are keen and engaged.

'They genuinely want to change their life around, they want to be there. They're eager and happy to learn, they like coming to the academy because it's a nice place to be.'

When Michelle went to New Hall she found it a lot quieter than she expected. 'I wasn't scared or anything – I'm not saying it felt normal, obviously it didn't feel normal – but I didn't feel on edge or anything, I didn't feel unsafe.' She expected to hear shouting and arguing because of what she saw on TV, but it was nothing like that. 'It's sort of like walking through a hospital.'

In terms of skills training, they do a lot of health and safety to start as that's the first thing to learn. Sometimes they teach different things at different stages so prisoners can help each other out and mentor each other. The workshops Michelle ran were based on photo ID, designing things and using the computers.

We observed that it seemed a little strange to us to teach prisoners how to cut keys and work with locks?

'Keys are actually something prisoners aren't taught until they are released and working in an actual Timpson branch. They tend to learn more about engraving and shoe repair rather than the keys and key cutting,' she replied.

Michelle enjoys the success stories and seeing ex-prisoners, who make up between 10 and 12 per cent of Timpson's workforce now, doing well in branches. Many of them go on to be managers or area managers and have risen above their circumstances. 'We have people throughout the company that have come from a criminal background… They're all successful because they've turned their lives around.'

Places are limited in the workshops, so only people guaranteed to be released are given one. Having too many people in the workshops with no prospect of prison release would take away places from those who want to go out and work after their sentence. Sometimes prisoners might not meet the criteria for the workshops, but this can be discussed with them and they might be able to join in the future if their behaviour improves. If they go to the Timpson Academy, prisoners are guaranteed a work trial upon their release.

Michelle told us that New Hall staff are 'really positive about the academy being there'. She described relationships with prisoners as 'natural' and just like a normal working relationship. Prisoners often speak about their personal lives and family. 'You've got to have a level, a line that you don't cross, but as long as those boundaries are acknowledged it can be really positive. They are prisoners, but they are colleagues.'

Policy at Michelle's branch states that only offences related to arson (due to Timpson's public liability) or to do with children, who often come into branches for photos, would mean someone would never be able to go to the academy if their offences related to these crimes. Michele pointed out that you could be working next to anybody who has done something and not been convicted: the only difference is that these people have been caught. She said she was always open-minded and still is.

* * *

Wakefield has other facilities, too, including a shop, a gym and a multi-faith chaplaincy. Our contributor

Martin Baker worked in the gym and brought many memories from there to us.

The segregation unit, the special unit, they didn't use the gym at all. So what I did was I managed to negotiate to put a running machine, a bike and a multigym down there. It was caged in at the bottom and they [the prisoners] could be let out one at a time, so one could be on the fitness machine and one could be on the bike and one could be on the multigym area.

Those that were on the segregation side – they could go back to a normal location after they'd finished in the seg. This gym wasn't for them but for the special seg unit, for those who were never on normal location, e.g. Robert Maudsley, Charlie Bronson etc.

It sounds strange but really they had quite an easy life down there. They had their breakfast, they had a bit of education or gym, exercise, visits… In my opinion it was too easy.

Martin used to see Levi Bellfield in the gym quite a lot.

'You could recognise him from that picture we have all seen in the paper as that's the only one they have of him, but he wasn't a big fat person. I think that was taken when he was on remand. When he first came to Wakefield he used to come to the gym before he changed his name [to Yusuf].'

Martin recalled Bellfield as always very pleasant.

'He was a typical psychopath. He came over very

decent, would always give his name if asked for it [even though everybody knew who he was].'

Martin initially joined as a PO. When the other gym officer left, Martin soon became the manager of the gym. He told us that you get an allowance to run the gym: maintenance for machines, for kits, for footballs, for weights, for dumbbells etc., for annual safety checks. When he started there, he had a 3/4k budget and when he left the gym, he had a £22k budget because he'd managed to bring things in and made positive changes.

For example, the first class of the day was remedial. Anyone with a physical injury could come and get help, but also anyone with mental health issues who wanted to work out to improve their mental state. The second session of the day would be cleaners after their early-morning clean before the meal. A lot of them also worked in the servery serving meals.

After lunch, kitchen workers came: they'd done all the work in the kitchen preparing lunch and it was then time for exercise. In the evening, anybody could come and exercise. Badminton, table tennis, volleyball, basketball, five-a-side football. There could be up to forty people lifting weights and on machines.

Martin had a diploma in the treatment of sports injuries so he could help prisoners by practising sports massage therapy on them, as well as hot and cold therapy and some advanced mobilising of joints. We wondered if it was a common area for incidents, but he assured us there were actually very few.

A maximum-security prison runs around five main things: wages, visits, canteen where they can buy things, physical education and association – where they're out, they're all unlocked, the whole wing, and they can associate. They're your main issues, so gym was very important in that. If somebody messed about we could take them off their class, we wouldn't ban them but we could take them off their class, they then had to reapply, which might take a month for a space to be available. So people didn't want to lose their space.

If people got jobs, they might be able to only go to the gym certain times than when they weren't employed, so a space would open up. It could be quite a quick turnover to get someone back in the gym if they were taken off.

You did get the odd skirmish but nothing major.

Martin played football with the prisoners quite regularly, too.

We'd play inside five-a-side, we'd play basketball with them, volleyball with them, and outside on the pitch we'd play with them. And in some instances, we've had staff–prisoner matches. I've also played in staff vs prisoner rugby matches... It was mostly the staff [who won the football] but sometimes you'd get some really good football prisoners come in that made the difference.

* * *

Throughout the UK prison system, and HMP Wakefield and HMP New Hall are no exception, all prisoners are subject to mandatory drugs testing. There are also voluntary testing arrangements, which become mandatory for inmates who are working cooking in the kitchens or cleaning on one of the wings.

Despite having mentioned drugs several times during our meeting with him, Jim reflected that Wakefield would probably have a lower level of drug usage than other prisons due to its high proportion of sex offenders. Stereotypically, a prisoner convicted of paedophilia or other sexual offences would be less likely to be using hard drugs.

However, even though the number would likely be less than other high-security prisons, drugs should always be something to be considered when managing a prison; there is a danger of power 'drift[ting] away from prison staff to the drug dealers in the prison' which Jim worked hard to prevent. When Jim first began his career in the early 70s, he notes that drug usage was unusual at the time – in part his was because there were fewer drugs and so it was less prominent – but it became a much larger issue in the 1990s.

During our conversations with Jo, she corroborated the notion that drugs had begun to emerge as a much bigger problem in recent history, and we can see why all Wakefield's drug screening was necessary. She told us: 'Tennis balls used to be thrown over the walls with drugs inside. They also put liquid cocaine on paper, and used cocaine for drawings. Now they use drones.'

This practice is part of the reason that Wakefield has put 'helicopter netting up'. According to Jo, 'Spice is the drug now.' She remembers an extraordinary device from her time at New Hall, the 'Boss Chair', which was used to check if anyone had any phones or other contraband in their crotch.

Pete gave us a great deal more useful context about drugs and other contraband.

'Plugging' was the most common method of sneaking in contraband. Shoving drugs up the anus or vagina, and then going into the visiting room, taking them out, putting them in the mouth, going in to see the prisoner and transferring the drugs through a kiss. The prisoner will swallow them and then several days later when they had passed through the body, they'd take them out of the toilet. Or they'd keep the drugs inside their mouth – if confronted they'd swallow them.

In the early days most common drug snuck in was cannabis – this was before mandatory drug testing (MDT). Cannabis stays in the system for twenty-eight days, whereas opiates is only five days max. The detox is three to five days, so if people came in saying they were addicted to cocaine, if you lock somebody in a room for five days, they would detox. It'd be a horrendous time for them, but they would detox. The only one you can't detox like that is an alcoholic – that's really bad, it's got to be done medically as the prisoner could die.

Other than drugs, people would sneak in money. They used to have 50 pences for the canteen, so they'd try and sneak in 50-pence pieces. There would be bookies on the wing who would loan out tobacco, which was the main currency, and then prisoners would owe them the 50-pence pieces. He then added:

Prisoners used to string 50 pences together and try and get them down the cavity in the brick, between the brick and the window on the outer wall, and that was on bunk laces. Genius some of the stuff they did. And they used to make models and have secret compartments in them that they used to put stuff in, they were brilliant stuff that we found!

Back in those days, prisoners were paid in money, if they worked five and a half in a workshop they might get six quid, paid it, and then they could spend that in the canteen and purchase goods. The main purchase is tobacco because most prisoners smoke. [Golden Virginia in ounce packets and they'd get quarter ounces, etc.] You could get a loan of baccie off a barren [dealer prisoner] but would always be 50 per cent interest— if you were loaned a quarter ounce, you'd have a half ounce to pay back etc.

They'd also bet on the horse racing and place bets with bookies and get odds.

You just allowed it to happen because it kept the lid on the place, giving them something to do. It were knowing your jail craft. But if any issues/bullying arose you'd give

them a tug and you'd pull 'em in, and then you'd rip the
cell apart, take all the money off them and take all the
baccie off them and say 'This ain't happening.'

Jenny witnessed drug use when she was inside: 'I remember going into one girl's room and she was smoking spice. She was a proper "rude girl", people were scared of her, and I've gone in there while they were smoking spice. I don't mind talking to anyone but she respectfully was like "You don't smoke so I'll stop." There was a real sense of understanding from people.'

She told us that contraband gets sneaked in all the time on visits.

You'd see people go in for a quick kiss or they'd go to
eat a bag of crisps and they would put something in the
bag of crisps and then pass it over and they'd take it out.
Sometimes it'd be so blatantly obvious.

Sometimes, they'd leave stuff in the visitors' toilets
and the prisoners would then come to clean the toilets,
where they'd collect contraband from. People brought
drugs and phones in all the time.

I spent the last eleven months of my sentence in
lockdown and the prison was still full of drugs. No visits,
no one left their room. Drugs were being sold more than
ever then. Officers would sometimes bring in drugs.
Girls got the drugs around during the twenty minutes'
exercise they were allowed during lockdown.

Another prisoner was authoritative on the current situation with drugs.

Drugs in prisons today – spice or legal highs as they were once known were smuggled in on visits and in royal mail bags. The twenty-four-hour Recorded Delivery silver bags you can buy from the post office. The hem on the bag would laced with spice and rolled over and superglued. The drug was in the hem of the bag. Censor staff would never open those bags using the hem to open, as when they are sealed the design is they cannot be opened using the hem again. Therefore they would be ripped open, checked with the whole bag and contents given to the prisoner.

Spice is actual tiny, minute wood shavings sprayed with the drug. To get high one would use specs of the spice into a roll-up. For one roll-up the price is £10. The effects are very bad as it is so strong. Back then, maybe five years ago, the prison service dogs were not trained to pick up the scent of spice as it was a new drug. However, as time moved on the smuggling techniques were discovered by the prison.

The spice, as said, is effectively a liquid sprayed onto tiny wood shavings. As the prison service discovered the smuggling techniques, the techniques of the prisoners changed. The liquid can be purchased online legally for £150 per litre. Prisoners would get their families to buy this and spray or soak an A4 sheet of paper in the liquid, let it dry, iron the page flat and print a letter on the laced page. This went through the prison censor department with ease. The profit is mind-blowing. An A4 page is 21cm in width, one line, which is 1cm in depth, is worth £210 inside prison. A 1cm strip is £10 to buy inside.

Inmates use their vape pens. Within the vapes [that go in the vape pens] is a small heating element that gets very hot. The vape is stripped to reveal the heating element and then inserted back onto the vape pen. It effectively becomes a small pipe. The 1cm of paper is cut up using nail clipper into tiny pieces. Little specs, like pin heads, that is how small it is and all you need to smoke. These are placed on the vape heating element and the vape pen is turned on. It heats up and burns the paper and smoke appears. The smoke is inhaled and you get high. It is like a little pipe. Wholesale one whole page can be sold for £1,000 easy. Even paying a £1,000 the profit can treble when cut into lines. 100 per cent of the prison drug trade now is paper-laced spice. HMP W, as with all prisons, has been flooded with this.

Spice is a game-changer within prisons. Prisoners with no real means will do anything, assault others [hits], sexual favours, steal, anything to get high. If a person has an issue with another prisoner, or even staff member, the dealer will just give them a line to attack the prisoner. A line of writing paper laced with the drug. Life and the safety of staff and inmates alike is so cheap now in prison. The prisoner who has been paid to carry out the attack will simply wrap up the line (his payment) in a plastic bag, insert it in his backside *to ensure that when he is overpowered by staff and taken to the segregation unit he can retrieve and smoke it. It is a nightmare for staff to tackle this issue. Small pieces of paper are very difficult to find when searching. Recently here [at HMP Frankland], only three months ago [November] a prisoner was seriously assaulted on the VP wings. An offender paid another with spice paper to assault the prisoner. It was brutal. The victim had his throat cut open, staff had to travel in the ambulance with the victim as they could not remove their hand from the victims neck as his main artery was severed. He died twice on route and went through a long surgery to save him. I have witnessed many of these near misses, but they are never reported on.*

Spice has changed so much in prisons. HMP W is known to be one of the most dangerous prisons in the system now.

With terrifying episodes such as this taking place, discipline is paramount. A regular, well-trodden and almost militaristic regime is necessary for the safety and security of all.

Chapter 4

Prison Regime

As Jo had informed us, everyone in Wakefield is following a regime. Either standard or enhanced.

Both standard and enhanced offenders have the chance of in-cell TV through the Incentives and Earned Privileges system. The better behaved they are, the more stuff they get. People say, 'Oh, they're not going to be bothered', but yes they are: to lose privileges like more visits, more spend, to be able to go to the gym, have a job, that's a lot – that's your life. But not to a psychopath. They couldn't care: basic, standard, whatever.

A seasoned Wakefield prisoner gave us a detailed and utterly compelling description of how the daily regime runs inside Wakefield.

Regime Mon – Friday, 8.30 unlock for work, main moves as we call them. Every wing mixes on these moves. You walk off the wing on to the workshops or education department. At 11.30 you exit the workshops or education; prior to leaving your location every prisoner is searched and subject to being wanded with a metal detector. In some cases you can be strip-searched. As you walk onto the wing you collect your dinner from the servery. A cold dish such as a ham roll, packet of crisps and a small child-like soft drink in a small carton. At 12.30 you are locked up. The prison will do what we call a 'roll check'. On the cell door is a small observation spy hole. Staff will count every prisoner to ensure none have gone missing. At 2pm, prisoners will be unlocked for main moves to work. 4.30pm prisoners will return to the wing and again be locked up for a roll check. Another headcount. 5.15pm prisoners will be unlocked to move freely on their wing. This is called association time. Mix with other offenders, play games, shower, just mix and chat. At 6.40pm prisoners will be locked up for the night, there will be another head count.

Only if you are a category A prisoner from then on throughout the night until the next morning you will be checked every two hours by night staff. A count is done every two hours. This to ensure you are still in your cell. For further security checks staff will conduct daily LBBs [Locks, Bolts and Bars]. LBBs are when staff walk into every cell each day and check your door locks and bars. To do this they have a rubber mallet and they will hit your bars and walls to ensure they're secure. By example, if you had by some miracle [impossible] cut through the window bars, when they hit it hard then surely it would be noticed. This is done throughout the prison system using the same technique. This can be frustrating because you end up with your cell being covered in black rubber marks on your walls and windows.

Mon–Fri is really a repetitive regime except on a Friday afternoon. The prison working week ends at lunch time on a Friday. At 2pm on a Friday, the wing will be unlocked for association until 5pm when you are locked up for the night. Weekend regime is simply unlocked at 9am, association, then locked up at 12 midday, roll check, unlocked at 2pm, association until 5pm, then locked up for the night and another roll check.

For our female prisoner Jenny, the schedule ran on some similar lines.

The first week, or two weeks max, you're locked in your cell and you don't get a job. When everyone else goes to work you're locked in. Then you'll get a job after that initial period. Weekly you'd get a little pack for breakfast. Tea bags, sugar, coffee to have in the cell. You'd go down to breakfast to get toast and they'd give you milk to add to your hot drinks in the cell and a pack of cereal.

The daily regime is very well organised. Jenny continued:

Around 8am unlocked, jump in shower, have breakfast, go to work around 9am. 11.30 to 11.45 go to lunch. Locked away for forty-five mins, then back to work in afternoon. Then come back around dinner, have dinner, back to rooms at around 6.30/6.45 and locked in for rest of night. Sundays you'd get unlocked in the morning, 8.30, and then locked away 11.30–12.30. Then allowed out all afternoon 2–5pm. Then locked in 5.15 onwards all night on Saturday and Sunday. Weekends were dead as there wasn't really much to do. Different wings had different privileges. The weekends we dreaded because Saturday, Sunday you were locked in your room 5 o'clock and there's nothing on TV, so it's crap unless you have a DVD player.

From a former governor perspective, Vanessa knows the typical schedule of a prison as well as anyone.

All prisons have a regime and the main aim is to stick to it. The night finishes around 7am and the day staff come on, who take over from the night staff. There are certain things you have to do; back in the day prisoners used to get breakfast – now they get a breakfast pack with everything they need the night before [carton of milk, cereal sachet]. Prisoners make their own. I don't miss the days of having to make the breakfasts: boiling eggs, making toast. They were fed up of burnt toast!

The first thing that staff do is 'count the landing'. This involves making sure they have all the prisoners, all accounted for and well. The first thing after that is exercise. Every single prisoner is entitled to an hour of exercise per day and except for exceptional circumstances they have to make sure it's given to them. The layout of this is different at every prison. There are different exercise yards for different wings.

So, to start the day she would unlock the prison, unlock the prisoners and send them off to exercise. Prisoners could refuse but the option was there.

'It is interesting, they all walked around the same way. You don't tell them which way to walk, but they all walk round the same way, that's all conditioning.'

Once back from exercise it's the start of the main day. If prisoners are convicted they have to work – if they refuse they can be put on report or even sent to segregation. Unconvicted prisoners don't have to work, but most unconvicted prisoners will want to go to the gym or education. If their literacy and numeracy is below a certain standard, they will be put into classes to get them up to an acceptable level. They have to go to education if this is the case. They go off to their various regimes, courses, classes, work and so forth.

The activities go on till lunchtime when the prisoners come back to the wing and grab lunch. Then they're locked up for an hour whilst the main body of staff go off to have their lunch break.

After lunch it's the same regime as the morning again.

Teatime they come back again, they have their main meal, and they are locked up again for 30 to 45 minutes for the staff dinner break. Then wings are unlocked for 'association' where everybody can mix with everybody (you need enough staff for this to happen safely), you can make phone calls, have showers, get stores etc. Sometimes there are evening education classes or gym activities. At half seven they are locked up again and staff do a final check, head count and then handover to the night staff again at 8pm.

'If you have one incident, say somebody, God forbid, commits suicide or attempts to commit suicide, we've got to lock all the 343 other prisoners away, so you've got to focus everything on one prisoner, but, however, you've still got those 343 other prisoners to deal with, to make sure they can make their phone calls to their family, to make sure they can have their dinner if they haven't had it yet.'

Essentially, you are forever juggling focus between prisoners.

John was, like Vanessa, extremely helpful and informative about daily life in prison, and he was able to describe the typical daily schedule within Wakefield Prison from a different perspective.

The day begins between 7:45–8:15 am. There will be a morning roll check where everybody will be counted. Cells are then unlocked and prisoners and officers are informed of their routine for the day. Prisoners will then attend their various jobs, classes, behaviour programmes and appointments. Once the morning has finished, prisoners will attend lunch, then are locked back up, and another roll call is conducted. For an hour to an hour and a half, the staff are given a break. At around 13:30pm, another roll call is carried out, the prisoners are unlocked again and continue their activities as before. In the evening, there is an evening meal. Depending on the day, there may be scheduled activities in the evening. The prisoners are then locked up again for the night between 7.30 and 8pm, where they will be secured for the next twelve hours with their television and phone.

Of course, Wakefield is a very high-security prison and so the category A and B prisoners would experience far more security than a lower-level category D prison. When John started working there, Wakefield was the highest security prison in Europe. One of the main differences John noted is the high number of roll calls to ensure prisoners are in the correct place at all times.

Both of our contributor Paul Powell's parents worked in the prison service and he wanted to follow in their footsteps. He applied to work at Wakefield because it was close to where he lived, and he had always wanted to work in a high security prison.

'There was probably a little bit of mystique around high security.'

Paul was posted at F wing: the segregation unit and did his first two and a half years there.

'It was a really great jail. Great to work at, great staff, very friendly, very welcoming.'

Wakefield was a completely different environment to other prisons.

'Wakefield is a lot more laid back, a lot quieter, less intense an environment to work at. I knew it had a good reputation and it didn't let me down. The regime was very structured around work, education, offender behaviour programmes, things like that.'

His wife Lisa recollected standout elements of the regime as part of a wider conversation about her experiences when she started work at Wakefield, and concurred with many of Paul's impressions. She already knew about Wakefield, because she originally wanted to be a dog handler when she joined the service. She had already been taken around Wakefield by the dog handler.

'I knew Wakefield but I didn't know how difficult it would be as a female joining a male establishment.'

Wakefield was very daunting because it was Lisa's first time in a 'proper prison' with the landings and traditional set-up, compared to Styal, which was set up more like houses than landings. 'Coming to Wakefield from a very busy female prison, Wakefield was a very relaxed atmosphere by comparison.

'That took a lot of getting used to. Styal prison had alarm bells going off very regularly, whereas at Wakefield you very rarely heard the alarms go off. I didn't feel a frightened atmosphere or anything like that, I just felt like it was a bit of a shock at first.'

On a typical day, there is a staff briefing first thing in the morning to fill staff in on new information. Wakefield was on a much larger scale than she was used to, and 'the regime has to be completely different' compared to other types of prison. 'The regime has always been very good at Wakefield. In the days leading up to my retirement, the staff run the prison as such and prisoners took to that because they need routine, they need regime. They're there for a long, long time – some of them will never get out of prison.'

When Lisa began, they had no integral sanitation. With no toilets or sinks in the cells, it was buckets. The prisoners would come out, empty the buckets, clean the buckets and take them back in after morning unlock as signified by the big centre bell.

'The smell used to be horrendous.'

Then it was on to the servery for breakfast. When everyone went off to their tasks – work, visits, classes – that whole turnover took just 20 to 30 minutes for all 700 or so prisoners.

Two cleaning officers on each wing would run the wing. They would make sure laundry was done and everything was clean, fetch any supplies needed or deal with complaints. Other staff were searching the wings. Lisa puts the smooth operation of Wakefield down to its dedicated staff.

Prisoners at Wakefield can work, including charity work, and there is an accredited course they can do in industrial cleaning. Education has a high premium placed on it, too. The Manchester College operates the Education department and offers a wide spectrum of learning, where offenders can do everything from learn basic skills to study an Open University course. Jo told us more about the sort of jobs different prisoner could do.

> *They work in the kitchen in Wakefield. They have workshops. Certain Cat As could work in an area but they couldn't go beyond. Cleaners on the wing: that was a really trusted job. The number one orderlies would clean the office… People stay at Wakefield. Although there is not a minimum four-year stay at Wakefield anymore, people are long term.*

We wanted to know if Jo was ever left alone with dangerous prisoners.

> *There were so many bad prisoners in Wakefield that you can't say, 'You can't come into my office!' There was not enough staff. If a psychopath came to my door, I would say, 'Hang on' and come out of the office onto the wing. I don't know whether psychopath's the right word? You just know someone that you wouldn't be alone with, that probably they don't care about killing you. A serial killer wouldn't just come in your office and kill you.*

This seemed like a very high-stakes risk assessment to us!

> *As an SO you would call them to your office, because they had some mail from their solicitor. You would call*

them in, make them sign for the mail, make sure there was no contraband in it and then you gave them it. It would just be me and him. You wouldn't have the staff for more than one officer there anyway. It was only when I left Wakefield that I thought, 'Oh, that's strange. A serial killer in my office...'

* * *

When asked about the typical daily schedule within women's prisons, our contributor Dr Maria Adams, who we introduce in full later in the book, stated that this would inevitably vary within prisons. From her experience, the prisoners would receive breakfast packs in the evening, and eat those the following morning instead of being let out for breakfast. Around 11am would be lunchtime, and after that prisoners would go to work or education classes. She noted a real emphasis on ensuring that everyone was involved in some form of purposeful activity.

All of the women prisoners were encouraged to do the basics for GCSE English and maths, but there were also diplomas that prisoners could take, as well as other practical classes such as carpentry, business studies and art. At around 4pm, they would have dinner. Something that struck Maria in her research was that timings for meals were very disconnected from the timings of the outside world; the schedule of the prisons operated around the food schedule.

Jo told us that nothing happens when a prisoner has a birthday. In a break from the usual monotonous routine, though, she said that in both Wakefield and New Hall, on Christmas Day and Boxing Day mornings they would have a lovely full-cooked breakfast – bacon, egg, sausage.

On Christmas Day there was a full Christmas dinner, including a halal choice, vegetarian, [and kosher] for a Jewish prisoner on one of the wings. They serve soup and then everything: the whole Christmas trimmings, Christmas puddings. Staff went off at 5 o'clock and, with a skeleton staff, prisoners would have a 'picnic box' – sandwiches, slice of quiche, Christmas cake, that would come out from the servery.

As a demographic aside, she recalled 'fewer than five Jewish prisoners in Wakefield. I can't think of any Chinese. No Jewish that I can remember at New Hall, not practising Jews anyway.' She continued:

When I was Acting SO at New Hall, you would be in the servery managing prisoners as they came through. If they were like 'Miss. I ordered this', it was like 'They ain't got it so get something else!' If you were in Wakefield and they said, 'I ordered so-and-so', I remember going there and I was saying, 'They ain't got it!' One of the officers says, 'No, Jo, you've got to actually ring the kitchen and see if they can go and get it.' Whereas the women just had to take what food was left, like a few vegetables. It was really bizarre.

At New Hall they got their dinner sheets a week

earlier and had to tick what they wanted to eat. If they didn't put it in it would be a non-order. In the male prison, if they didn't put it in an order, you had to leave what was there and they could choose what they wanted... In New Hall, and I think Wakefield too, you'd have your pamphlet the prisoners got over Christmas and New Year: 'We're having a quiz, we're having this and that.' I'm sure they could win money on their phone cards and stuff. My dad used to say to me, 'Don't tell me!'

A prisoner's description of the food, however, makes it sound a little less sumptuous in nature.

Food is served on the twos landing and each wing has a built-in serving hatch. You walk in one door, up the line of the serving counter and walk out of another door. This is located on the left-hand side as you walk onto the wing opposite the senior officers and CM's office. Breakfast serving is done the night before when you collect your supper. You are given a pack of cereal and a small milk. The milk cartons are tiny and hold 189ml of milk.

Jenny was quite well-treated by staff at her prison, in her view because 'It depends on you. If you give an officer an inkling of attitude, they will not support you. They'll be rude, they'll make your life hell.' She feels that she was treated quite well. She saw officers support women who were upset and crying, so they could be supportive.

She also saw officers 'be assholes' but only to people who treated them badly first.

> *The first year was horrific, it was so tough being locked away with my own head… There's nothing to prepare you for prison. Now it's changed, but when I was a prisoner I had a job where I would greet the newbies and tell them everything they needed to know and how to survive etc. When I went into prison, I didn't have that. It is quite refreshing when you get into prison as there are some prisoners you trust more than some officers. Half the officers don't know their job anyway. No one prepares you.*

She recalled her terrible first night in prison: 'I was scared. I was terrified.'

Her and her partner came into the same prison. They had a chat that they would have to pretend not to know each other and keep their heads down. The officers saw them together and ended up putting them both on the same ward, 'so that played out well'.

> *You have to do twenty-four hours' watch in a single cell when you first go in. All night a woman was kicking and screaming, you know that ain't someone being naughty, that's someone with mental health, because I wouldn't have the energy to do that. And I was thinking, 'Oh my God, is this a mental hospital, what am I going to wake up to?' I was terrified of the unknown… If no one's*

screaming, you can hear a pin drop at night-time. But as soon as the doors open it's like they've let the animals out the zoo.

She didn't want to leave her room and get food. She had preconceptions in her head about prison.

'I always thought it was like the movies. I'd heard that Holloway girls got raped. I only had two fears and that was death and prison – but I still carried on selling drugs! You gotta fight for your life. I thought it'd be violent, terrifying.'

She recalls loads of groups of people.

'The rude girls, the little dinky kids that you just want to mother, drug addicts, what you would call the norm (me).'

You were allowed to bring personal belongings in.

If you have jewellery on, you can keep a set amount on. No big hoops. You can have a necklace, watch, ring, but that's about it. But you have to already be wearing it. You can't have it sent in after. Footwear you're allowed two or three pairs, not high heels. Sliders are useful for the shared showers. Five pairs of bottoms, two shorts, twelve tops and then more if you were an enhanced prisoner.

She didn't really see instances of bullying 'unless you were a dickhead and brought it upon yourself. The minute you start giving an attitude people will switch on you.'

She said that camaraderie and friendships in prison are so important in prison, 'one hundred per cent'.

INSIDE WAKEFIELD PRISON

It is like a little family. When people are struggling, people will really come together and I think our main support comes from prisoners, it doesn't come from the system. Everyone really does look out for each other. It's the mother instinct in people. I got on with everybody. Would spend time with the 'baddest' girls, the ones who sold drugs, and would then go and hang out with the most 'geeky' girls. Everyone kind of talked to everyone.

Chapter 5

The Training

John Hartshorne is a recently retired prison officer, who spent the majority of his thirty-three-year long career in Wakefield Prison, but with plenty of experience working across the country in other institutions, including New Hall women's prison. We have already met him in Chapter 2, explaining prison categorisation to us. He began his career in 1989, when he left the Royal Navy, joining prison work in October that year. Whilst his work took him all over the UK, he was predominantly based in Yorkshire.

He's progressed through the ranks and has done a range of jobs, from prison officer work to government, security, headquarter and rehabilitation work, and with that comes decades of experience dealing with prisons, from category C through to A – one of his most notable moments was being present for the 1990 riots at Strangeways, Manchester. The final ten years of his career centred around successful work as a trusted figure with female prisoners, which he considers to be both rewarding and a great privilege, as many have suffered trauma at the hands of men.

John philosophised that 'we are products of our early experiences.' Having been bullied throughout his early life, he had developed skills to manage himself in difficult situations, ensuring 'I was only bullied once by each individual'. He always stood up for himself and seemed unable to walk away. Whilst at first this got him into some 'tight squeezes', his later work in the navy allowed him to develop healthier coping skills.

The appeal for John in prison work came from his familiarity with heavily male-centric environments. However, when he joined the prison service, the industry was undergoing critical change with the integration of more women workers. Whilst many long-serving male officers were set in their ways and resented this shift in the workplace, John welcomed it and saw it as a positive change. Overall, John sought the uniformed and policed environment that he had grown accustomed to during his naval service, hence working in prisons fulfilled that need.

When he left the navy, with a young family, John accepted the first thing that came along. A prison officer role at Wakefield. Despite living locally, he was unaware of the prison's reputation before he started his application. It was only when the process was underway that a few friends working in similar institutions were able to give him some preparatory insight into what to expect. He completed an application form, written test and then, as part of a whittled down group, an interview with three men.

The questions that were posed to him during this interview were 'interesting' and strange. It started off with fairly straightforward questions. Had he ever been to prison himself? He had not. He was then asked what he imagined prison to be like, and he drew comparisons with his time spent on an aircraft carrier.

John was asked if his wife would mind him having to work night shifts occasionally. Having come off seven months at sea, she was patient and used to him being away. It was at this point that the questioning became very personal. One of the interviewers asked:

'You haven't got any male friends have you, nipping around to see your wife when you're on nights?'

John was shocked by the question, and angry at the implication that his wife might be cheating on him. Despite this 'ridiculous' interaction, John explained that he handled himself well. In hindsight, reflecting on his later experience, John was sure that the interviewers were deliberately trying to jab him to see if they could provoke a reaction, preparing him for the fact that many prisoners he would interact with would attempt to do the same. If he couldn't handle it in the interview, or resorted to anger or violence, he certainly wouldn't have been able to handle working inside a prison. Although, John laughed, their goading was 'very gentle' compared to what he would later experience.

The entire process from application to hire took about eighteen months, then John began his time at training school, preparing for his work as a prison officer. Prior to formal training, the recruits were sent to a training school for a nine- to ten-week period to better prepare them. John was based at Wakefield for this period and was in a class of around twenty people for this introductory course into prison work. He described the process as very full on and 'quite tortuous at times'. As part of this training, recruits were sent to report to a prison for two weeks, shadowing another officer. During that time, the new hires were given a notebook, and had to keep a very detailed daily report.

Questions included how many prisoners on B wing that morning, routines, how many people came downstairs, how many category A prisoners, B prisoners, where were the emergency exits, fire bells and alarms, and so forth, all testing observational skills and dedication.

Wakefield prided itself on its heavy-duty preparatory work for its officers before training, with an expectation they would go on to surpass their peers later in formal training.

In a key moment from his early days, John was working on A wing, and the prisoners were working at their different jobs. One of the prisoners was the head cleaner for that wing and coordinated the other prisoners on cleaning duty. The head cleaner made tea for the officers on duty that day; due to his 'inexperience and naivety at the time', John had refused because he thought that he, a prisoner, might tamper with the officers' drinks.

The other officers on duty then asked the same prisoner to cut out some cleaning signs to use in the toilets. John noted in particular that the officers seemed to make a big deal of the fact that the prisoner was using scissors: 'You've got over that now, haven't you? That was a long time ago.'

Then, as if to unnerve the new trainees, the prisoner described that one of his long-lasting memories of his wife was when 'the scissors were going in and out of her eye sockets'. John was unsure as to whether this was legitimate, but it seemed too well planned, elaborate and spontaneous for it to have been a sick joke.

'If you get into that environment and it gets under your skin it can be very difficult to shake off.'

To work in a prison, John noted that your personal and mental resilience needs to be high. John's clear communication and ability to tell people bluntly 'how it is' also put him in good stead. He may not have been the most eloquent, but he was always fully transparent.

Another aspect of the job is being able to remain objective. John explained: 'If you speak to [prisoners] I think you'd probably find out that a third of them are completely innocent, the other third haven't done exactly what they've been locked up for, and then there's another third that don't give a monkey's about what anyone thinks about them – you ask about what they've done, and if they got another chance they'd probably do the same again.'

Regardless of what prisoners attempt to condition people to believe, they have been found guilty in the court of law, and to John that's what you have to accept. John was shocked to see, unlike in the navy, officers or prisoners would often refuse to do something when asked, something completely alien to him. Although, when he became a supervisor, he did come up with a very effective method to get officers to comply.

If a member of staff would refuse to do something, John would invite them into his office, print out a copy of the job description, give them a highlighter and ask them to tell him which part of the job description they couldn't do. There were never any problems after that. John noted that 'you can't force feed people experience'. He would never ask someone to do something he wouldn't do himself and would often lead the way, allowing for well-rounded learning experiences and giving people the chance to develop.

* * *

Our contributor Lisa, having joined the prison service in 1987 at Styal women's prison, was also happy to share her training with us. Lisa went to Wakefield in 1989 until she medically retired in 2013. She finished as a prison officer, working through all the ranks to get to that role. She worked in every department: 'I think I know every brick within the wall.'

When Lisa joined Wakefield there were only three other female staff working there, one from Holloway, one fresh trainee and one caterer. Until around that time, women had worked in women's prisons and men had worked in men's prisons. Mixing had only just started. Although she emphasised it is very different now, then, she added, 'it was pretty bad to be perfectly honest'.

*I came into a very male-dominated atmosphere, [both]
staff and prisoners. We didn't have our own toilet, we
weren't allowed a locker, because the lockers were all in
one big room, where the male staff are. We were only
allowed to work in certain areas of the prison, tending
to do jobs that a lot of male staff didn't want to do.
Whether it was to protect us I don't really know, but
we could only work with certain levels of prisoners. We
weren't allowed to work on landings where there were
category A prisoners… Our toilet was in the chaplaincy
department, so if you needed to use the toilet you had to
go all the way to the chaplaincy.*

Lisa and her Holloway colleague had both come from
some of the most violent female prisons at the time. They
were well experienced in handling difficult prisoners.
'I had to prove myself physically and emotionally that I
could handle the men.'

She was given more 'female' jobs, like supervising
workshops, or 'a prime example: on visits we were just
allocated handbag searching.'

The male staff could be tricky, too, with the majority 'very
hostile. They didn't want female staff there.' Some were
probably threatened by female staff, others felt protective of
the female staff and didn't want them to get hurt.

'Some felt it would spoil their male-oriented conversations. Some would be nice as pie and asking questions,
they'd be telling you all about their wife, girlfriends,
children, and then you'd hear, "I've been in effing workshop

with split-arse over there", and yet ten minutes ago they were absolutely lovely to your face.'

Female officers were charmingly called 'split-arse' by male staff as a common nickname. Fortunately, attitudes changed with the increase in female staff – psychologists and probation as well as officers. Some old-school officers retired, replaced by males less resistant to female staff, and good friendships with male officers, who would then subsequently support Lisa as a woman in the field, helped too.

You had to prove yourself in a male-dominated way physically. I had come from a busy female prison where we were restraining prisoners daily. I was involved in an incident [at Wakefield] where I had to restrain quite a violent prisoner with other male colleagues. It changed for me then. It was like pat on the back and 'Ooh you can handle yourself.' You had to work twice as hard emotionally to prove that you could do the job, deal with prisoners and stick up for yourself with staff.

Lisa recalled that 'every single [staff office on the landing] used to be covered from floor to the light bulb with page three girls, of centrefolds, so you had to work in that office seeing all this and dealing with sex offenders at the same time!'

* * *

Our contributor Martin Baker was a more recent Wakefield arrival, but still very much a veteran, having started in 1999 as an SO in the PE department. He was promoted to PO on discipline, being designated part of the orderly officer group. There were six principal officers who covered the jail 24 hours a day, 365 days a year. They looked after the day-to-day running of the jail. Dealing with any incidents would take nights, days, and they'd have to sort incidents as soon as possible. He was promoted to governor grade manager F, then went back to PO. At sixty he went down to SO and worked on the gate part-time.

Like John, Martin was ex-navy, having been a Royal Marine Commando. After working in several other prisons, he moved to Wakefield with his wife.

Wakefield was always something different. When I went to Wakefield, I'd worked in other prisons full-time and I'd worked in a number of prisons on detached duty. A lot of people I met at Wakefield have never worked anywhere else, so they didn't know there was another way of doing something… people didn't want change, didn't like change… When I first went to Wakefield there was a centre bubble, and on the centre there was a bell. So you rang the bell 'ding' and everybody unlocked, you rang the bell again 'ding' and everybody went to work. You rang the bell again and everybody locked up. It was all done on a bell. Tik tock, tick tock.

The bell was subsequently disposed of and it would operate with phone calls; the wing would call the ECR [Electronic Control Room] and alert them they were about to unlock etc. Martin calls; practices like that 'grossly old fashioned. They didn't even use bells on Her Majesty's ships where they all originated from. It was disciplined because there were a lot of sex offenders and staff liked it disciplined because it bred safety.'

When Martin joined, they were refurbishing the wings one by one. They widened the staircases, and gradually modernised it.

'You can have the most modern prison in the world, but if you've got old thinking... What I saw everyday was brilliant, it worked superbly, but that didn't mean it was right. It was very old fashioned in its thinking and it was difficult to get it screaming and kicking into the twentieth century.'

Martin spent his first few days at Wakefield figuring out where everybody was, how the radios worked, 'stepping back and seeing how high-security prisons worked in their day to day with a higher security on movement'. He had to record every movement and ask permission for every movement by phoning ECR. At that time, dogs accompanied movements for Cat As before they scrapped that.

'I liked working with long-term prisoners because you get to see the same guy everyday for ten years. So you see the same types of people, you know their foibles, you know their moods, you can see when they come in what sort of mood they're in. You can talk to them.'

The orderly officer group that Martin was in was disciplined, and in charge of the day to day running of the regime. That meant ensuring that people were unlocked, or at work on time, or going to seg on time. He had no issues with anything in the jail.

'If something went wrong, or an alarm bell went, we had to get there first to be in charge.'

It was his job to ensure that everything and everyone was in line: staff and prisoners. If a prisoner was in an area they shouldn't be in, he made sure they went back to the right place.

'We were very much the eyes and ears around the jail. If things weren't happening as they should or if we saw something was wrong, our agenda was to deal with it there and then and try to put it right.'

Martin used to take the governor around on his rounds. He once took the governor up on the fours and there was a staff member with his feet up in a comfy chair watching TV instead of working: 'Staff are fickle, if they can get away with something they will.'

The governor said, 'Do you reckon you should give him a bollocking?' to which Martin replied he probably should. 'Do you think the whole jail should hear it?'

'I gave him my best Sergeant Major and tore a strip off this lad. The officer's little office was right at the end, right by the centre, so it reverberated round all four wings, the tea room and everywhere else!'

Martin does not recall seeing much mistreatment of prisoners. What would happen was if a prisoner needed something and a staff member was busy, they might tell them to wait ten minutes, even if the staff member was not really busy.

'Prisoners don't like hearing the word "no", or don't like hearing the word "wait", it infuriates them and gets their back up.'

Or, say a prisoner has diarrhoea and has run out of toilet roll and asks for more. A good member of staff would give one straight away, a bad member of staff might say, 'Give me ten minutes', but in that instance a prisoner can't wait. Martin would step in and say, 'That's not on.'

'Don't put yourself in a position where people can make complaints about you. Some people will do it out of malice, some will do it out of laziness, some will do it because they can. Some people are conscientious and would never do it. You've got to get everybody up to the high standard.'

* * *

We wanted to know all about Pete Wightman's training, too, of course. Pete joined the prison service on 14 July 1986. He did training, and went to Wakefield to start with for a week. He then went to Newbold Revel for officer training. He spent eighteen months at a category C prison in Cumbria before getting a job back at Wakefield as he really wanted. Pete made an observation that Martin had also made, that the service was transitioning from very disciplined and militaristic to less so during this time. For Pete it seemed like a fresh start.

Financially it was tough, because the maximum hours contracted were forty-eight, including nine hours of overtime. Pete did twelve years at Wakefield, where he was promoted to senior officer and then principal officer. He worked a lot in security. He worked with police and DNA testing and with the IRA 'which wasn't very nice'. He worked as a wing officer, wing senior officer, and in security. Alongside all of this, Pete worked in the segregation unit a lot with prisoners that included Charlie Bronson, Douglas Wakefield, Robert Maudsley and Reginald Wilson: 'Nasty pieces of work.'

He moved from Wakefield to New Hall in 2000 until 2004 and then moved to Leeds where he subsequently retired in February 2019.

'I really enjoyed my first fifteen years in the service,' he told us. 'I hated the end of it, couldn't wait to retire, and I wouldn't join now.'

We wanted to know what changed. According to Pete, the lack of discipline changed massively, and there was a massive staff reduction. Now, overall across all prisons, in his experience they are 'appalling places to work'. Pete had some preconceptions about Wakefield.

'I'd just heard it were full of nasty people. But they were in a confined environment and on a very strict discipline regime.'

In terms of the training at Wakefield, on the first day you met the governor and walked around the establishment. The trainees were all in suits, staff all in uniforms.

'Chief officers [the role no longer exists] were the

ones who disciplined staff – governors didn't have much of anything to do with the uniformed officers. We were "screws": the prison term for officers.'

He observed that Wakefield also had 'a hell of a lot of Cat A prisoners and sex offenders. Lots of category As who needed escorting and were on books and needed to be signed for when moved and received. Forever trying to sneak where they weren't supposed to.'

In terms of other violence: 'Wasn't many assaults but when there was an assault it was a bad assault.'

Could any of this extensive training, for any of these individuals, prepare you for an encounter with Wakefield's longest-serving and most infamous inhabitant, Robert Maudsley?

Chapter 6

Robert Maudsley

Often described as the real-life Hannibal Lecter, Robert Maudsley has been kept in a purpose-built underground cell in Wakefield for over four decades. He is one of Britain's most dangerous killers, murdering only sex offenders and paedophiles, and will never be released. He earned the nicknames 'Hannibal the Cannibal' and 'Spoons' after a spoon was found sticking out of the brain of a prisoner he had locked in a cell for nine hours and tortured with a fellow inmate whilst at Broadmoor.

For our Broadmoor book, we had an exclusive interview with one of the first nurses on the scene at this gruesome crime. This is what he told us:

In a nine-hour siege inside the little corner of hell resident murderer Robert 'Bob' Maudsley had created, Bob and his companion, David Cheeseman, had sealed themselves inside with a third patient, David Francis, a known paedophile. He had apparently riled Bob and David Cheeseman by conducting a homosexual attack on one of their friends. David Francis had been hog-tied with a record player flex and tortured throughout the interminable deadlock in the claustrophobic, airless unit. Burly and grizzled as the Broadmoor nurses tend to be, they could not break inside Bob Maudsley's room. Eventually put out of his agony with a makeshift garrotting, he was then paraded in front of the cell's spy hatch for the helpless Broadmoor staff to see. When they finally gained access, the victim was partially skinned. This flaying had likely taken place while he was still alive, as his screams echoing through Broadmoor during his ordeal had testified.

One of the first nurses on the scene described to us 'sperm coming out of every orifice' of the victim. He has asked us not to reveal his name, and he is still traumatised by the experience decades later. According to another staff source quoted in the press, David Francis was discovered with his head 'cracked open like a boiled egg', a spoon hanging out of it and his brain partially absent.

After being declared unfit to stand trial, Robert Maudsley had been sent to Broadmoor hospital and remained there for three relatively uneventful years before this incident happened. More than forty years on, this 1977 incident remains perhaps the most notorious crime to take place within Broadmoor's walls – and there is certainly plenty of competition for that dubious honour.

* * *

Today in Wakefield Prison, Maudsley is kept in confinement for twenty-three hours of the day. Everything in his cell is made of cardboard and you have to go through seventeen steel doors to get to it.

The tabloid press have been integral in keeping the mythical status of Robert Maudsley alive. A journalist contact of ours, Charles Wade-Palmer, who has broken a couple of our scoops, wrote an article about Maudsley that was pretty much a greatest hits of the legends about him, but what was the truth behind it?

Starting as he meant to go on in his 2023 article, Charles understandably led on the most sensational aspects of Maudsley's story.

Robert Maudsley has spent 40 years in total isolation, inside a specially-constructed glass cell below HMP Wakefield.

Deep below the ground at Britain's 'Monster Mansion' is one of the country's most dangerous criminals, dubbed 'The Brain Eater' by fellow inmates.

Grim tales of Robert Maudsley's cannibalism have surrounded his time behind bars – and the twisted serial killer's existence in jail is eerily similar to Hannibal Lecter's in the film Silence of the Lambs.

Authorities had to have an underground glass box cell specially constructed for 'Hannibal the Cannibal' Maudsley, who had previously killed three fellow prisoners and threatened to strike again in a letter to his nephew.

The brutal killer has now broken a world record for the length of time spent in solitary confinement – 16,400 days, or almost 45 years.

Most of this has been inside his bulletproof dungeon below HMP Wakefield, a prison dubbed 'Monster Mansion' due to its high-risk population.

One prisoner contact was more than happy to reminiscence about Maudsley, and his fractured relationship with Charles Bronson.

Robert Maudsley – Bob as he is known – hates Bronson, they simply do not get on. When I was on the unit, RM would play rock music loud to wind up Bronson. Given he was next door to him the music would penetrate through the wall. Bronson would shout at him. However, RM would never reply.

RM does not use the gym on the CSC, he is odd in the sense he has never communicated verbally with other prisoners; when on the yard he will just slowly walk around the yard ignoring others who are on the other yards. He is no trouble to staff at all.

Our contributor Jo expressed shock that Maudsley was serving his sentence in the conditions that he still is.

He's been in the CSC – the close supervision unit – since I was there! Six officers and an SO to unlock him. God, all he did was kill a couple of bloody nonces! Child killers. And they put him in there! He had a list apparently of all the nonces he wanted to kill. And it's like, 'and?' He's an older guy. Six on top of him and a senior officer? Why? And he admitted to it! He went to the cell door and said, ''Ere boss, you're gonna have two off your roll check!' They were like 'What? Lock down', and they found them under the bed [as we describe above].

Jo also had a disturbing story about another example that she witnessed of Bronson baiting and tormenting Maudsley, on the basis of his childhood abuse.

His mother was vile to him. It's said she locked him in the cupboard and whistled… I remember going on the CSC and it wasn't my wing: I was on C wing and then I changed over to the A wing for about two and a half years. I'd come from New Hall. I was walking, whistling and they were saying, 'Ma'am you can't whistle.' I said, 'You what? You're telling me not to whistle because it upsets a con?' It was just weird. He hated Bronson and Bronson hated him. Bronson used to whistle sometimes.

Maybe not put him on normal location because he could… but just move him to the other side, to the seg – three officers to unlock you.

93

Pete was very familiar with Robert Maudsley. He referred to Maudsley's solitary confinement cell as 'the strongbox'. Pete gave us lots of fascinating information about Maudsley and was very much of the opinion that Maudsley would kill again if released.

'The sad thing is, if he were living with someone else, he'd kill somebody else. It'd have been more humane to just put him down.'

When it comes to the Perspex cell that, legend has it, Maudsley is kept in, every contributor tells a different story. Pete, for example, described the box in the following terms: 'Metal with thick Perspex around them that looked out into the middle and there was a metal door with thick Perspex on it and then an outer cell door. They were boxes.'

As he described it to us, it was all completely see-through, except from the front of the cell: 'You could lift the flap up and look in. But you could walk in between the two [there were two of these box-like cells] and there were thick Perspex and metal framing as well. They were secure units; they couldn't get out.'

In summary, the secure accommodation, or strongbox, was:

'A cell with a concrete plinth in it, and an industrial blanket and an industrial dress that we used to put him in. If he kicked off and assaulted somebody we'd put him in there until he'd calmed down. Or, he'd ask the SO to go in, if he felt his head were going.'

Pete explained that there were two strongboxes side

by side. Maudsley was in one of them and had plenty of prisoners in the other cell next door that would come and go. They can see each other through the clear Perspex walls.

They used to share a television and would take it in turns to pick what to watch. It was only up to about 8pm, not like nowadays where they can watch TV 24/7 as they have TVs in their own cells. If Bob [Robert M] picked Monday, then he would pick Wednesday, Friday, Sunday etc. and would roll over every week. If he was in there by himself he could choose every night. If he and his neighbour didn't get on, they might stop him from watching shows he liked during their days to choose. Even if they wanted to watch the same things, they might do it to annoy him. Robert Maudsley liked to watch Emmerdale *and* Coronation Street *and his neighbour would deliberately change the channel just as they were coming on just to annoy him.*

Then he could only watch them every other night, when he had control of the remote. There was no catch-up TV back then, either. Pete told us that Maudsley didn't tend to get on with any of his neighbours really, and likewise they didn't get on with him. Staff were very cautious of Robert Maudsley.

'Because he would have killed you and not blinked an eyelid. He killed anyone he got close to. And he wouldn't have gotten any extra time because he's doing natural life. There was always an SO and six further officers to unlock Robert.'

Pete spoke to him every day. He described him as a 'big strapping fella'.

He'd have days where he were really quiet, and there'd be days where he would ask for stuff because he used to do a lot of drawing in his cell. He used to do Braille as well for the Braille unit at Wakefield. They'd give it to him, just to occupy him. They never used it because he couldn't do it right, but it were just giving him something to do... He'd write letters, he'd draw, he used to watch TV in the evening and do a hell of a lot of Braille.

As Pete tells it, Maudsley was not friendly to staff, 'he were another nasty piece of work'. With a seemingly hierarchical approach, he was more open to conversation with the 'higher ups'.

The governor used to do his rounds every day and he'd speak to the governor; if he wanted anything he'd ask the SO or the PO. He didn't come out of his cell, his meals were taken to him. So, you used to go down with the SO and six to unlock his outer door to put his food in. When he'd come out for exercise, you had to search him again, starting from his head, check his hands, rub him down and then escort him out onto yard.

Pete described that for Maudsley they also used to also have an Alsatian dog, known as a 'Zulu patrol' unit, to come out with him. Maudsley had to exercise by himself as he couldn't be around others.

Of course, Maudsley's reputation, and his 'Spoons' nickname, preceded him with Pete. 'He earned the nickname "Spoons" because he allegedly killed a guy in Broadmoor, cut the top of his head off and ate his brains with a spoon.'

Maudsley was always in the box when Pete was at Wakefield, where Maudsley had murdered Salney Darwood and William Roberts in 1978:

When he killed them, he'd have a shiv, a blade that he'd made in the workshop. He went in the cell, killed the prisoners, and then the bell went for lockup. He'd run out of time. He had more people that he were gonna kill. He went to the office, and they were in the middle of the wing. And he threw the bloody blade into the office and said, 'If you go into the cell so-and-so, I've killed him, and if you go to cell so-and-so, I've killed him...'

Pete recognised Maudsley's mental health issues and felt that nowadays he'd see a psychiatrist and be on medication [as he would have had at Broadmoor], but it wasn't dealt with in those days in that way in prison. 'He committed those crimes and they just shoved him in a box and forgot about him, because they didn't know how to deal with him, they didn't know what to do!'

* * *

We asked Vanessa about the rumour that Robert Maudsley was kept in a Perspex box, too. She emphasised that she did not know for sure, but having kept in touch with lots of people in the service, she has heard rumours.

'I have heard that he is kept in a specifically built glass box; he is the longest serving prisoner in solitary confinement, and that is because he is a danger to others. You can't take the risk of him doing it again [which] far outweighs the fact that he is in solitary confinement. He probably has in-cell activities to keep him amused: education, books, TV. I would imagine he has because if you just shut somebody in a box and left them, they'd literally go mad.'

Vanessa told us the story of a female Holloway prisoner who was sent to solitary because she posed a danger to other prisoners. Every night she would fashion a garrotte that she would keep under her pillow. Every day they would remove it and every night there would be a new one; she was waiting for a prisoner to pass her and she'd jump out. She loved the staff but really resented other prisoners.

'To release her into the general prison population would have been seen as a failure on the prison's part to the general public, that we didn't protect whichever individual they ended up hurting.'

In the context of Maudsley but also on a more general note, we asked Vanessa to go into a bit more detail describing the conditions of solitary confinement, which she explained usually happens in segregation units.

'Segregation units are often split into two categories. Half is for punishment, half is for segregation to protect the prisoner: if they're in debt to other prisoners, or they might be high profile or a celebrity.'

Vanessa described fifteen prison rules. If these are broken, they can be put on report, and the person overseeing this can decide up to a maximum of twenty-one days solitary confinement or cellular confinement.

Whilst in that punishment confinement they have no TV. They're allowed a book and some personal possessions. They get an hour's exercise a day but they don't mix with other prisoners. It is treated as a breaker of a cycle of their bad behaviour or habits. As Vanessa remarked:

'Sometimes a short, sharp shock will suffice.'

They are visited by a governor daily or an independent board, or by a doctor or nurse to check on their wellbeing, but that's it.

'It's a useful tool, solitary confinement.'

* * *

We talked about Robert Maudsley to our contributor Martin, too. Martin told us that he only really interacted with his personal officer, and for a very dark reason.

'That was the problem with him, wasn't it? If you got close to him, because of the way his parents had treated him, if anybody got close to him that's when he killed them.'

99

According to Martin, Robert Maudsley was fairly 'unkempt' and didn't really come out before they installed the multigym down there with access from his strongbox – this is a cell with a raised area for a bed and – like those cones that come out the ground to stop cars going by – it was fixed concrete for sitting on.

In an act of desperation in 2000, Maudsley begged for an easing of his solitary or to be allowed to commit suicide with a cyanide capsule rather than spend the rest of his life inside in solitary. After a five-day hearing it was dismissed, and he remains in Wakefield almost a quarter of a century later.

After the hearing, Maudsley wrote a despairing letter to a newspaper which included the words:

What purpose is served by keeping me locked up 23 hours a day? Why even bother to feed me and to give me one hour's exercise a day? Who actually am I a risk to? As a consequence of my current treatment and confinement, I feel that all I have to look forward to is indeed psychological breakdown, mental illness and probable suicide.

Geoffrey Wansell, a renowned true crime author, shares this sense of the tragic aspects of Maudsley's plight, considering the frail old man he is today.

'He is virtually unable to walk. He's like "Hissing Sid" [Hissing Sid is Sidney Cooke, another very long-term inmate we discuss in Chapter 9]. He is a massive victim of the system. Maudsley has become a totemic figure in the prison system. I feel infinitely sorry for Maudsley. He says, "Why don't you let me kill myself?" That is very difficult to answer.'

Perhaps the only other Wakefield inmate, past or present, with the same notoriety is his former foe in segregation, Charles Bronson.

Chapter 7

Charles Bronson

Entire books and films have been dedicated to the extraordinary, violent life of Charles Bronson. We wanted to get first-hand testimony from people who had never fully told their stories about him before, particularly, of course, stories from his time at Wakefield Prison.

Britain's most notorious prisoner has been in and out of Monster Mansion countless times over the years and has compared it to London Zoo. In 1993, he even spent forty days naked in isolation there.

We have decided to refer to him as Charles Bronson in this book as that is how he was known at the height of his 'fame', but he has, of course, been through a number of aliases. He was born Michael Gordon Peterson on 6 December 1952. He embraced the name Charles Bronson, after the American action star, when his bare-knuckle boxing promoter suggested that he adopt it in the late 1980s. After converting to Islam many years later, he changed his name to Charles Ali Ahmed. Since 2014, he has been known as Charles Arthur Salvador in homage to his favourite artist, Salvador Dalí.

In addition to the time he has spent at Wakefield that we will be focusing on, he has done time in all three of England's high-security psychiatric hospitals: Broadmoor, as we have described in our previous book, Rampton and Ashworth. Though, as he has stated himself, he has never killed anyone, his history of extreme violence has been enough to lock him into a sentence of life imprisonment. He has attacked both fellow prisoners and guards on numerous occasions, and he has been a hostage-taker in the past.

As with everyone that we spoke to about him, Geoffrey Wansell finds him a thoroughly intriguing character.

'Charlie Bronson, or Charlie Salvador as he is known now: how do you put him into the spectrum [in terms of likelihood to reoffend if he was released]. He'd probably have to go back to prison within fifteen minutes!'

Geoffrey and Emma agreed that the flamboyant aspects of a character like Charlie make a very welcome relief from the heart- and gut-wrenching stories of rapes and murders that the true-crime writer has to engage with. As Geoffrey said, 'You get a bit tired of grim.' How does he get through it?

'Each case illuminates something.'

One of our prisoner contacts was not a fan of Bronson, and gave us an enthralling account of how irritated he was by the hype around him:

The CSC unit is where Bronson is held when he is at HMP W. You would have read and heard the stories that he is held in a cage, this is utter nonsense. Lies, lies, lies. Anyone with an ounce of common sense would surely conclude we are in the European Convention and there are human rights issues to consider here. It would just never happen. I spent a year in the segregation unit and on the CSC unit in 2013. The seg and the CSC unit are next door to each other. Indeed the seg conditions are worse because they are punishment conditions whereas the CSC conditions are long-term living conditions and not considered a punishment regime.

I was fighting a criminal case when I was in the segregation and I needed electric to power my laptop. I was therefore moved into a CSC cell next door to Bronson. His cell has a TV, a telephone, nice furniture, a bed, his own private bedding. The CSC has its own gym, right outside his door. Luxury showers, music playing while he is in the gym. On the other side of Bronson was Robert Maudsley, who killed other inmates in HMP W in the 80s... Bronson, and this is the truth, is like a spoiled child. He moans and moans when he does not get his own way.

He is actually on the CSC for his own protection because he is a target due to his own media campaign when claiming he is one of the UK's hardest offenders. The truth is, yes, when he was younger he was a handful, this is true. However, he is now just a little old man. He dyes his tash black, which actually looks *ridiculous. He wears those hideous dark glasses for show. I argued with him, he hates being called Micky Peterson; I told him what right-minded man changes his name to Bronson, after a 1980s film character? I told him his art is childish. He tells inmates he is from the East End of London, I reminded him he is actually from the sticks in Luton. He made many threats to me that he would kill me if he got me, of course I just wound him up. Some brutal facts about Bronson, he does not live in a cage at all.*

He came to prison for robbing a ring from a shop. Any person with an ounce of common sense would have just served his time and got released. However, he took a weak, polite art teacher hostage and got a life sentence. He has completed no offending courses, been obstructive to staff throughout, and in any event could never locate on normal location because he fears he will be attacked. He is no victim nor is he hard done by. For his age he is fit. He does use the gym every day, he can even cook his own food. He has a TV, DVD player and an Xbox. The image the media present is simply untrue… His social visits are even more private, he gets his own room whereas other offenders have to share a packed room. He is currently housed at HMP Woodhill, in a lovely unit… They even have their own chillout room with bean bags and huge TVs and video games.

All the above is fact and a true reflection of his life.

The prisoner went on to give even more intriguing specifics about Bronson's daily life now.

Bronson, or Salvador as he now calls himself, does live an isolated life away from other inmates, however he does interact with staff on a daily basis. An example of his daily routine is as follows: he has access to the gym either a.m. or p.m., the gym is directly outside his cell door. The gym is inside a huge cage type area. He will be locked in the gym area and left. The view into the gym is clear through the bars, it is not in an enclosed room. The gym has free weights, a multi gym, bikes and rowing machines. There is a treadmill too, the equipment is very good. After the gym he can shower. The showers are private, however there is a barred gate at the entrance and he will be locked in the shower while he is in there. He can then have exercise, either a.m. or p.m. The seg CSC unit has six exercise yards. They are all caged-in, set outside. He can take soft exercise mats out on the yard with him if he so chooses to do so. These can be used for training or to lay in the sun. Many use them for both.

On the unit you can also use the self-contained library. There is a small education room on the unit and a visiting room. There is a small kitchen area where he can cook if he wishes. However, in every area on the CSU you will be locked in the area you are. This is for your own and others' protection. No offenders on the seg or CSC regime can have contact with each other while you are located there. Bronson will communicate with other offenders by shouting out the windows at night or during the day. This is how they communicate. General chats. Magazines and newspapers can be passed to each other via staff.

As we have seen, our staff contributor John has come face to face with some of Wakefield's most notorious prisoners on many occasions, and Charles Bronson is no exception.

On one memorable occasion, John was involved with the transfer of Charles Bronson from HMP Wakefield to HMP Frankland. John refers to him as 'Charlie'. On the day of his transfer, Charlie had refused to wear his prison clothing, and so was transferred whilst wearing nothing but a towel and a body belt. There were three officers and a senior officer escorting Charlie; John had sat in the back with him for the duration of the journey. Upon departure, the senior officer gave a speech to Charlie:

Right then, Charlie, just before we go out the gate, we got three officers here, two in the front, one driving, one navigating and one in the back [John]. Like everything else in life, there's a hard way and an easy way to do things. We've got a couple hours' drive. If you're happy to spend these two hours on the floor of the van, and me and these other three sat on top of you in the most uncomfortable way, then that's one option. Or, we can sit down and have a bit of a crack and a bit of a laugh.

Charlie opted for the latter, regaling the officers with stories from his youth. John looked back on the memory fondly. 'It was a great trip!' One story that stood out to John, though he stressed he cannot vouch for its accuracy, was the story of how Charlie was sent to prison. He had been planning to rob a bank, and was sat in his car preparing himself. John reflected that Charlie had painted an almost caricatured image of a robbery he was involved in.

'I don't know if he [Charlie] had gotten his bank robbing ideas from *Boy's Own* or some other thing, but he expected to go in there with, I don't know, a bag saying "SWAG" on it, and say "Fill the bag full of money" and run out.'

Between him bending down to pick up his gun and looking up, Charlie found himself surrounded by police officers and was subsequently arrested. Charlie then confided to John, 'All I wanted was a bag of money!' John surmised that 'his planning wasn't really up to scratch'.

John discussed the importance of keeping such high-profile prisoners away from 'normal location' prisoners.

'The only way that you can have a bigger influence than Charlie Bronson, as far as notoriety is concerned, and crime and prisons, is to be the person that killed him.'

Although Charlie was a handful, he continued, 'it's nothing that we can't deal with and nothing that we haven't dealt with before!' When prompted as to the problems caused by Charles Bronson, John recalled a time he had been sent out as a negotiator to talk with Charlie. He had refused to come in from the exercise yard.

'I can't remember what his demands were, but they usually involved a helicopter.'

In the past, Charlie had supposedly taken hostages and got other prisoners involved in his demands, but John had found that the best way to deal with Charles Bronson was to wait.

'You just wait him out until he gets fed up. It's usually around lunchtime.'

On the other hand, Charlie had also been known to get on well with some of the officers, and would often spar with one of the them who enjoyed boxing, 'because he's a human being. He's not a bad person.'

Our contributor Lisa echoed the positivity towards Bronson that we were picking up from virtually all the staff we met who worked with him, unlike the loathing coming from some of his fellow prisoners. 'I never had an issue,' she said. 'He was always polite with me, nice asking questions. It would depend a lot with Charlie on what way the wind were blowing.'

The slightest thing could affect him. He had select staff that he built a rapport and had good banter with.

'He was no real problem to us at Wakefield but everyone is aware of how dangerous he is.' When meeting more notorious prisoners such as Bronson, Lisa went on, 'what I always advised my staff to do was to go and read their record. So you've got a little bit of a background about them.'

Lisa's philosophy was to try to treat all prisoners the same – almost all of the prisoners in Wakefield had some form of media attention, so to treat them all the same, never single one out from the others etc.

Lisa fondly recalls prison banter and how 'it would make our day go a bit quicker and a bit more enjoyable. Staff and prisoner rapport was always very good.' Indeed, she can't really think of anything that she really disliked about the job, apart from the early days where her integration as a woman brought issues.

Her husband Paul, however, had very different impressions after he first met Bronson in 1987 when he came to Full Sutton: 'The angriest man I've ever met. So angry with everything and everybody.'

Paul recalled that Bronson assaulted three members of staff on D wing at Full Sutton and was shipped out. 'I was working in the segregation unit one evening [at Wakefield] and he turned up. This van appeared and he was on it.'

Charlie recognised Paul when he arrived at Wakefield and when he first saw him said: 'What are you doing here?'

Paul responded: 'Well Charlie, I could ask you the same question. I thought I managed to shake you off when I left Full Sutton.' CB started laughing.

'He could be alright, he could have you in stitches, but he could be extremely intimidating and extremely angry. He was generally alright if everything was going his way. But when he didn't get what he wanted or he didn't like what he heard, it got a bit... testy, shall we say. Very volatile. He's got a long history of assaulting staff.'

Paul offered the kind of insight we love on prisoners watching their own publicity, and their reaction to it.

'I remember they split up [Bronson and his wife] and she did an interview on TV and they let him watch it, they gave him a television so he could watch it, which was a bit odd, because obviously he's quite a volatile person, but he took it pretty well, to be fair.'

We wanted to ask Paul about Bronson's artwork, too.

'He used to do drawings and sometimes he'd shove them out under his door for you to have a look at. It's what he did. He's obviously a very good drawer... I think a lot of it used to be what was going on in his mind.'

* * *

We were fortunate to meet renowned author Robert Verkaik, whose books include the *Sunday Times* bestseller *The Traitor of Colditz*, for several reasons, but none more so than because we were fans of the extraordinary piece of journalism he wrote about meeting Charles 'Salvador' in Wakefield. We were not disappointed. When we met him he brought the encounter to life for us and gave intriguing nuggets of information that were not shared in the article.

There was a vetting process for admission and they sent someone round to vet him, but that individual never asked if he was a journalist. If you ask to go and see a prisoner nine times out of ten you won't get permission.

He told us that the day he visited Wakefield, he entered the reception centre at the end of Love Lane, where there were lockers to put your belongings in. He was then escorted through airport-style security by a prison officer.

Charlie had asked him for chocolate bars, so he asked the officer if he could stop in the prison to buy him some, and he did, Double Deckers to be exact, which he liked. He went through the incredibly long series of doors: 'If I said seventeen in the article it was seventeen!'

Then, 170 yards to the left, is the segregation unit, what Robert termed the 'prison within a prison'. Bronson shouted out 'Hello Robert!'

There is more security again as you go into the segregation unit. Robert noticed five or six courtyards outside each cell. Someone was exercising in one of them, who he thinks might have been 'Bob' Maudsley. Robert suspects that Robert Black was on the segregation unit at that time, too.

The guards walk you down into a big room. Bronson was in his own cell. Robert was in what was effectively another cell next to it, and even though it had a chair in it, it was impractically designed so that you could not sit on the chair and talk to Bronson properly. Robert basically ended up standing for the two hours or more that their meeting lasted.

Robert's description of his personality and demeanour chimes with the accounts of many others in this book.

'He's very captivating, a magnetic personality, and has a gift for entertaining people. He's old now though, he's got psychiatric problems. He had a ZZ Top beard when I met him, and dark glasses because he said years of segregation had affected his eyes.'

For Robert, his memorable meeting with Bronson

inevitably raised questions about rehabilitation and whole-life terms. 'He's old enough now that if he had a good record...'

We talked again about that interesting tipping point where an individual is arguably incarcerated because of what they once were rather than because of any real danger they might pose to the outside world as an old man.

'Bronson makes you think about punishment, and the right to redemption. He would clearly benefit from some consistent psychiatric help.'

Charlie gave Robert a rolled-up sheet of one of his drawings. Robert was keen to seem grateful for this, as he was aware that 'one of the people he kidnapped had not been enthusiastic enough about his art'.

Even so, Robert's praise was apparently not fulsome enough, because subsequently he received a menacing letter from Bronson that said: 'It's very rude not to thank someone when they give you a gift.'

Robert surmised that the guards really liked Charlie. He had built up respect. In Robert's view being a prison guard is a boring job and Charlie can entertain. We closed off the meeting wishing Robert luck with his latest book about the Battle of Arnhem, and felt grateful for the chance to get his input.

* * *

Pete worked with Bronson in the segregation unit because he wasn't on normal location, and recalls instances of extreme violence, much as Paul does.

'He loved to assault staff. He were a violent refractory prisoner. We used to receive him into the segregation unit and there were usually an SO and six to unlock, because you never knew when he would kick off, and he were a fit bloke. He spent all his days doing press-ups and sit-ups and pull-ups all in his cell.'

Pete mentioned to us that Mick O'Hagan 'had a good relationship with Charlie. Ex-military, ex-boxer.' Mick O'Hagan, an officer who has gone on record many times on this topic, first welcomed Bronson to Wakefield's F wing after he had gained a reputation for extreme violence in other institutions. Mick has described himself as pivotal in inspiring Bronson to reform himself and stop being so violent, by giving him his first sketchbook. Bronson subsequently created multiple books and artworks.

Pete remembered those artworks well.

'He used to draw you cartoons did Charlie. "Here you are gov, done this for you!" With his little black glasses. Everything was "sweet": "sweet gov" was his typical response to anything. He used to swear all the time. He were a bit of a character, but if he kicked off you knew about it.'

From his first-hand experience of the man, Pete is far less inclined to go easy on him than many others we spoke to.

'People saying, "Oh you should let him out of jail, he only went in for bank robbery, armed robbery." He took a teacher hostage in Hull, and he ruined that teacher's life. He were leading him round with a flipping piece of string around his neck. He should never be released. And if he were released now, even though he's a lot older, you'd have some young buck wanting to kill him to make a name for himself, you know, "I did Charlie Bronson over."'

Pete has vivid memories of Bronson's prison wedding, too.

'I can't remember what they called her. It was a marriage of convenience, she wanted to make a name for herself. It were absolutely ludicrous. He was allowed a couple of hours in the visits' hall with a few guests.'

Pete only ever had short conversations with Bronson as he was locked in a double cell: the box in the segregation unit. Pete spoke to him to give him his food, or ask him if he wanted something, such as any 'apps' – applications for letters.

'He didn't speak to officers, he only spoke to the SO or the PO. He wouldn't ask the staff, because they were below him. When he did speak to you it'd be "O-rite, Gov?" in a very strong cockney accent. "All screws are fucking bastards": he used to say that a lot.'

In addition to deploying such colourful language, Bronson could often be found causing trouble elsewhere.

'You'd get him out to go on to exercise, and he'd just hit a member of staff. He did quite like Wakefield. Because it's very disciplined. He got what he were entitled to, and plenty of it, but nothing else. And if he didn't behave himself, then he didn't get any extras. If he didn't conform, he couldn't come out.'

In Pete's view, Bronson had a very limited mentality and could not necessarily offer a reason for his actions.

'He would say, when he refused to come back from exercise, "Today's sunny, I'm fucking stopping out here, you can fuck off!" If he refused to come in, they'd go and kit the staff up and send them in with a shield where they would C&R [control and restrain] him and put him back in the cell.'

In the seg at Wakefield everyone had a locker with an extra uniform inside. Why?

'There weren't many days where you didn't get potted [see Glossary for description of this disgusting practice], or you didn't get food thrown at you, or you didn't roll around the floor with somebody. There may well be days where you might have five or six altercations with different prisoners in segregation.'

Pete confirmed what we had heard from many other sources, that for a time Bronson was kept in the cell next to Robert Maudsley. Bronson and Robert Maudsley had their own shower separate from the rest of the prisoners. As mentioned earlier, they had a television in between the cells and would take it in turns to choose the channels. Back then they would have to turn off the TVs at 8pm, unlike today where they have twenty-four-hour access.

Our contributor Martin met Bronson at Long Lartin, where 'he wasn't a particular problem', and was not on the seg, even if he did blow up occasionally, as Pete described above.

Charlie went on the yard and he wouldn't come back in. They got teams ready to go in. So for one person you had to have three C&R teams, which is nine people. But why go in and run around? So they called the national C&R and the team went in, Charlie ran at them and they pepper-sprayed him. And of course that took all the fight out of him.

His thing then was 'Blimey, you can't even have a fight anymore!' Why bother fighting when you can stop people in their tracks?

One of Martin's best Bronson anecdotes was from Long Lartin, not Wakefield, but it's so great we could not resist including it.

The alarm bell went one day. Martin and a PO went up and there was Charlie, covered in Vaseline, cammed out with black and green camo paint on his face and a bandana round his head. 'Come on ya bastards!' They quickly did a right turn into a 'trolley corridor' and got shields and things, but when he came out all he wanted was some medication to calm him down. The doctor came and injected him in the seg and then he was fine. He went back to normal location the following week.

Part of this behaviour and notoriety, as the prisoner contact who described Bronson's personality to us is convinced of, is self-styling.

Our contributor Vanessa did not meet Charles Bronson

herself but had heard the rumours of course. 'Charlie Bronson was named as "Britain's most violent prisoner". I don't know about that, I know he is violent but I've seen a few female prisoners that could wear that tag. That is the nature of the beast.' You never quite know how to interpret these rumours. How much is exaggerated.

There is a whole gangster subculture that forms around figures like Bronson. Perhaps the most suggestive comparison is with the Kray brothers.

Emma had reached out to the celebrity gangster Dave Courtney on social media and was awaiting a response when the tragic news came that he had taken his own life on 22 October 2023. He was suffering from both cancer and arthritis. He was found dead at his south London home, Camelot Castle. He was an affiliate of London gangsters such as the Kray brothers, Lenny McLean and Roy Shaw. He was just sixty-four years old when he took his own life. Poignantly, he had made eight videos on his mobile phone early in the morning of the fateful day. They included goodbye messages to his ex-wife, son and daughter, indicating that he planned to take his own life. It was one of his friends, Brendan McGirr, who discovered his body the following day and found him in his room lying dead on his bed.

Courtney started out as a debt collector, and apart from a conviction for possessing live ammunition in January 2009, he was never found guilty of any other offence. A charismatic character, he became an actor in gangster movies including *The Dead Sleep Easy*, *Clubbing to Death* and *Six Bend Trapp*. In the course of his film-making he built a collection of around seventy firearms, which had been decommissioned, or fired blanks.

Chapter 8

Colin Ireland

One historic occupant of the Yorkshire jail, Colin Ireland, intrigued us enough to warrant giving him his own chapter, not least because he provoked very different responses in different contributors. He stands out as one of the few people to have really rattled one of our seasoned contributors, Vanessa Frake-Harris, even though she has really seen it all, but others had a very different take.

Colin Ireland was a serial killer who murdered five homosexual men over a period of three months in the early 1990s, leading to the nickname the 'Gay Slayer' in the popular press. He died from pulmonary thrombosis in 2012.

But what did Vanessa make of him? Colin Ireland was the only prisoner she met of note and recognised. In common with the oddly domestic detail of many of the encounters with serial killers we describe in this book, she met him in the canteen.

They had a different canteen to most prisons where prisoners could order food or wander in. She was chatting to the guy who was showing her around, and as she stepped back she bumped into someone. She turned to say sorry and was struck suddenly by the fact that this was Colin Ireland, and when she looked up, he just kept on going; he was huge.

'He's probably the only prisoner that has made the hairs on the back of my neck stand up.'

He didn't say a word, he just looked through her. No emotion, no recognition. Most people would acknowledge someone in that situation but he just didn't. We could think of plenty of reasons, but with stiff competition in the people she had met, just why did Ireland unsettle her quite so much?

Vanessa explained. As we know, Wakefield was known as 'Monster Mansion' throughout the prison service. Even though she thinks of it as a 'bit of an unfair name', she knew the kind of people she would find there. These were people whose crimes were so shocking and despicable that they stared out at you from every tabloid during and after their trials. In addition, she originated from London and that is where most of Colin Ireland's murders took place, so she was well aware of him.

'He was very overbearing, you could imagine somebody of average build, average size wouldn't have stood a chance against him.'

Vanessa told us that she does not tend to think about prisoners' offences unless she is directly involved with them: for example, if she needs to write a report on one of them. Unless she specifically needed to know such details, she just didn't want to know.

'That's not my job; they've been tried and they've been judged by their peers. It was my job to keep them safe and secure.'

In the case of Colin Ireland, she had no choice but to be aware of what he had done.

Colin Ireland was born on 16 March 1954. As with Robert Maudsley, a terrible start in life and a dreadful upbringing led him into a life of youth crime and stints in both borstal and adult prisons. He then embarked on a horrific torture and killing spree, murdering five men and gaining the nickname the 'Gay Slayer'. He would target his victims, who he met at the Coleherne pub in Earl's Court, central London, in a careful and organised way, and he carried a murder kit of handcuffs, rope and a change of clothes. Purporting to be interested in a submissive/dominant sex game, once he had lured his victims into inviting him back to their apartment, he would torture and murder them. He would clean the flat afterwards and stay the night, taking an almost forensic approach to not getting caught.

On 20 December 1994, Ireland was sentenced to five counts of life imprisonment, one for each of his ghastly murders. He died aged fifty-seven, still caged in Wakefield, on 21 February 2012.

When we met her, Vanessa told us that she tries not to pre-judge, especially when visiting another jail. She believes that would be unfair to both the staff and to the prisoners. She was full of nothing but praise for the former: 'The staff do an amazing job at Wakefield and under difficult circumstances.'

In terms of the prison itself: 'Everybody knew that they housed the worst of the worst sex offenders.' Even so, and with the burden of that knowledge in her mind, her meeting with Ireland is seared into her memory as one of the most unsettling encounters in her long and successful career.

Our contributor Martin offered a wholly contrasting view of Colin Ireland when we spoke to him, describing him as: 'Just a bit of a big daft lad really... He was always a bit mouthy but he never pushed it past the point. Occasionally he was a bit dizzy, but basically he just used to try to bully people by verbals.'

Our contributor Pete had similar recollections: 'He were good as gold as a prisoner. Not a minute's trouble.'

In Pete's time, Colin spent most of his time on A wing, and Pete used to escort him to workshops because he worked in metal workshops. He was friendly, which was not as uncommon as we would have thought with inmates.

'A lot of them were very friendly, it were a closed community, you saw more of them than you did your family, because you worked that many hours. So, you did build up a lot of relations with them, not unprofessional but professional relationships.'

These relationships could reach a point where the prison officers were very attuned to the prisoners' moods.

You knew when they were up and you knew when they were down. They'd tell you when they got a visit, they'd tell you if they'd had a letter, they'd show you pictures and say. 'Oh boss, what do you reckon, that's my sister's child' or 'that's my brother's son' or 'My brother's got a flipping job in the police!' They were normal people. They haven't got three heads and sixteen legs. They are normal, everyday people, who have committed horrendous crimes.

Our contributor Paul was even more glowing, describing Ireland as 'always polite, always good with staff'.

Because Wakefield housed sex offenders, he felt these more notorious prisoners didn't have so much of a target on their backs because everyone who was there was in there for horrific crimes. 'They were all sort of like the same.'

Paul reflected on how the demographic at Wakefield might have suited Colin too.

'Colin Ireland was a funny one because he was obviously in prison for the murder of homosexuals. So he was out mingling in a prison full of people that he probably didn't like. But he kept himself to himself. And that's what a lot of them do.'

Jo told us that she wasn't threatened by him, either.

'I was SO sometimes on exercise. There would be two staff one end of the exercise yard, they just walked around, always anti-clockwise. In bloody New Hall they're so bone idle, you put them out on exercise and they're just on the floor or sat on the benches. E wing had an exercise yard. There was grass in the middle. As an SO, you'd be clocking everyone who came in. You'd have your Cat A books in your hand – I think they got rid of them. You'd be knocking your numbers off your roll board. Ireland was very tall. I always used to say, if I ever can't do my job because I feel intimidated, I'll leave. I wasn't ever frightened of challenging people head on.'

Levi Bellfield was on Jo's wing. What was he like as a presence?

'I've seen bigger. Levi is not that big. He's six foot something. Short hair. He didn't intimidate me.'

Jo says that she was not rattled even when she was on her own with him. 'Levi came into my office, just me and him. The only people you didn't have in your office on your own were psychopaths.'

She continued: 'You'd call a murderer or a rapist into your office but not a psychopath. There were more male staff than female in Wakefield. The prisoners all seemed to have people writing to them.'

* * *

Another inmate, Peter Moore, committed similar crimes to Colin Ireland, predating on the gay community. Between September and December 1995, he stabbed to death and mutilated four men. As one prisoner recollected to us:

Peter Moore I know very well. He actually writes to me now on a regular basis. He has some minor health issues but is in good shape for his age. A very tall man with a full head of grey hair with a huge 1980s grey tash. Although he is from Wales, he speaks very well [posh] in a London accent. He is very articulate, clever man.

Moore had told the jury during his trial that his crimes were committed by a fictional gay lover that he nicknamed Jason, after the serial killer in the *Friday the 13th* horror movie franchise. The jury went on to find him, rather than Jason, guilty on all counts.

As sick as it sounds, but you want the truth, he actually jokes about his crimes. He claims they were committed by his alter ego Jason. His favourite sick joke about his crimes are he once dressed in a policeman's uniform, stopped a car and tied up a couple, male and his female partner. He said the man pleaded with him not to sexually assault the woman, he then said, 'Sir, how dare you, I'm not here for her, it's you I want.' Peter actually thinks this was funny. I have spent hours with him and him revealing all the details of his crimes. His voice is so polite and professional, very well spoken, and it is so odd to listen to a well-spoken man talk so much horror. Not the sort of thing you would expect from someone so well spoken.

He is extremely fit. He goes out on exercise daily. He has no visits and when not working he cooks and keeps himself to himself. He must have some personality issues because when he tells his stories he will give the impression it was him that committed the crimes all the way through the conversation, then he will blame Jason.

This strange behaviour leads us on to another the story of another current Wakefield inmate who has seemed terribly amused by his own past crimes, Ian Watkins.

Chapter 9

Ian Watkins

Former rock god Ian Watkins had the world at his feet when he threw it away because of his perverted, paedophile obsession with children and even babies. Born on 30 July 1977 in Merthyr Tydfil, Wales, he went to secondary school with his future bandmate Mike Lewis. A talented artist, he was awarded a first-class degree in graphic design from the University of Wales, Newport. He co-founded the rock band Lostprophets in 1997, serving as lead singer and frontman, with Lee Gaze on guitar. Leading a seemingly charmed life, his band enjoyed success and he enjoyed the celebrity lifestyle, including a high-profile romance with British TV presenter Fearne Cotton in 2005.

We asked our contributor Martin about Watkins, who he said talked about his band but didn't talk about Fearne Cotton. He had a select group of people he hung out with. 'They all mix with like-minded people. There's not diversity; a gangster doesn't want to mix with a paedophile and a paedophile doesn't want to mix with a rapist.'

How did he look when Martin knew him? He had been rather striking when he was front man of a rock band: 'He had long straggly hair. He was a bit scruffy and if he didn't want to go to work, he didn't go to work, and he was getting nicked because he wanted to just laze about in his cell and drink tea.' But like anybody, he'd be forced out and have to take part in the regime.

In his life before prison, all was not what it seemed. Unfortunately, despite numerous red flags and reports to the police, he was free to commit grotesque acts of abuse on a number of occasions before he was finally brought to justice. Another one of his ex-girlfriends, Joanne Mjadzelics, was prompted to complain on multiple occasions to South Wales Police after he displayed graphic images to her of both children and drug abuse in 2010, but there was no effective police follow-up. She had also been made aware by the shameless Watkins himself that, while recording the Lostprophets album *The Betrayed* in Los Angeles in 2009, he was abusing a two-year-old child. Even though Joanne contacted the child's parent, and the parents had also reported his abuse to the Welsh authorities, again, nothing was done.

It later emerged that Joanne was one of six people who had contacted the police regarding their suspicions about Watkins between 2008 and 2011, including an Australian woman who accused Watkins of assaulting her child, also in 2010, but the authorities did not investigate the allegations further. Watkins appeared to have some sort of charmed, celebrity protective ring around him despite the gravity of the accusations.

Ironically, even when he was finally apprehended, in June 2012, it was for drug offences rather than child abuse. Welsh police had been made aware by some of Watkins' friends that he was smuggling coke and methamphetamine from Los Angeles. He was granted bail but then arrested again on 4 November 2012 for drug possession and also – a breakthrough – for possession of an indecent image of a child. After he pleaded not guilty to the charges of possessing such material, he was granted bail again, and, somewhat unbelievably with hindsight, even performed onstage with the Lostprophets on 14 November 2012 in his old university town of Newport.

Yet another drug possession charge led to his third arrest on 17 December of the same year. This, on top of their prior investigation, prompted a search of his home and computer by South Wales Police. The investigation was codenamed Globe, and they had needed to enlist the help of GCHQ to decrypt his concealed laptop drive, which contained evidence of his crimes. When investigators did manage to successfully bypass the encrypted password to his computer, his password was 'I FUK KIDZ'. Talk about hiding in plain sight! The failure of the police to act sooner on the accusations that they were presented with, which arguably allowed an organised and committed paedophile to commit many more crimes with impunity, later led to a lengthy Independent Police Complaints Commission review and report.

During the search, officers discovered numerous indecent images of children on his computer. With the pace finally picking up, just two days later he was being charged at Cardiff Magistrates' Court with conspiracy to engage in sexual activity with a one-year-old girl and possession and/or distribution of not just indecent images of children but of extreme animal pornography. Along with two co-accused females, he was remanded in custody, though his barrister insisted that he would deny the accusations.

On New Year's Eve 2012, he appeared at Cardiff Crown Court via video link from HM Prison Parc, Bridgend. He was remanded in custody, along with the two females. The legal process trundled along, with a trial date set for 15 July 2013; at a hearing the previous month he had denied the charges. Eventually, the trial started on 25 November, with an application for the court venue to be moved outside of Wales having been denied.

Watkins pleaded guilty to the attempted rape and sexual assault of a child under thirteen, but not guilty to rape on 26 November 2013. This was accepted by the prosecution. He further pleaded guilty to three counts of sexual assault involving children; six counts of taking, making or possessing indecent images of children; and one count of possessing an extreme pornographic image involving a sex act on an animal. Sickeningly, his victims included a baby boy. Even so, Watkins apparently saw a funny side, referring to his paedophile offences as 'mega lolz' in a phone call he made from prison to a female fan.

Presumably he was less amused when Mr Justice Royce sentenced him to twenty-nine years in prison, with eligibility to apply for parole in 2031, which would be followed by six years of supervised release. During sentencing, Judge Royce declared: 'This case breaks new ground. Any decent person... will experience shock, revulsion and incredulity.' A senior investigating officer on the case described Watkins as 'potentially the most dangerous sex offender' he had ever encountered.

He had previously been imprisoned at HM Prison Parc when he was on remand, but given what he had been found guilty of, Monster Mansion beckoned. Having started serving his sentence at HMP Wakefield, in January 2014 he was moved to HM Prison Long Lartin so he could be close to his mother after her kidney transplant. There, he was accused of grooming a young mother, writing her letters from prison, in October 2017.

It was not long, March 2018 to be exact, until he was back in Wakefield. In that same month, he was found with a mobile phone in prison, and a charger in his cell, which he was accused of using to make contact with a girlfriend outside prison. Watkins claimed that it was not his phone, but that of two inmates who had coerced him into hiding it for them, and who had threatened him with violence if he divulged their names.

He claimed that he still received fan mail from Lostprophets fans and that the men wanted to monetise the contact by taking advantage of females writing in to him. The case went to trial at Leeds Crown Court in August 2019, and he ended up sentenced to a further ten months in prison.

As we know from many other examples, rough justice is particularly likely to be meted out to nonces, the lowest of the low in high-security prisons. On 5 August 2023, three other prisoners in Wakefield took Watkins hostage, beat him and stabbed him, until he was freed by prison officers six hours later. His injuries were severe, but not life-threatening. Whether he is granted parole in 2031 will depend on a number of factors, not least whether there are any other incidents between now and then.

We heard first-hand allegations from one prisoner about the rough justice meted out to Watkins in Wakefield that confirm he doesn't seem to be having a very good time there:

Ian Watkins is currently located at HMP W [February 2024]. He was recently attacked and stabbed in his cell. He is a tall thin male who dyes his thinning hair black. The prison service actually sells hair dye. Watkins was a rock star who was part of the group the Lostprophets. He has access to money and spends his time buying his friendship. Money exchanges are easily done in prison. The person you're paying, you simply take their friends' or families' phone number on the outside, give that number over the phone to your family. They call the person outside and take their bank details and pay the money into their account. Watkins was caught with a phone. He had paid a Liverpool gang member £1,000 to use the phone, and when he got caught with it he had to pay £5,000. This is fact, I know the guy who lent him the phone…

Watkins is on C wing at HMP W. His work activity is education. He buys his protection and his recent stabbing was due to a drugs debt. He is considered vile amongst other offenders [because of his involvement in sexual offences against babies]. He pays for protection. He has many female fans and receives letters from a lot of females. He maintains his innocence because of the shame of his crimes. He is hated by many but as HMP W is mixed, i.e. VPs and high-level gangsters, drug importers and organised crime, they just take money off him for his safety. He has spent thousands on protection. The recent stabbing was a reminder that he needs to pay. He took an amount of spice off a prisoner with a prison value of £150. Because it was Watkins he was told he owed £900. He was high and refused to pay, therefore he was stabbed in the side using a sharpened toilet brush.

In our contributor Jo's view, Watkins' treatment needs to be placed in the context of the special treatment given to 'celebrity' prisoners, which can be better or worse than normal. She believes that Rolf Harris was given a tough time but that Savile might have had special treatment if he had been caught.

With Watkins…for some reason these people that go in that are high profile, like bastard Rolf Harris, I can't say they are treated softly. Like Savile wouldn't have been treated normally, it would have been 'watch how you do this, it's Jimmy Savile!' 'Oh, sorry, is he not a prisoner?' 'What you talking about?' 'He's a dirty, filthy, raping necrophiliac bastard. Yeah! Shagging dead bodies'!

Our contributor John actually knew Ian Watkins' victim. She had been locked up because she'd been manipulated by him and got them to help him. For John Watkins is an 'absolutely horrendous individual'. He wouldn't share her location. She lives under a different name and identity now. 'He did that. You could absolutely tell, despite the circumstances that she found herself in, she was a marvellous woman, but vulnerable. That man's ruined lives.'

In John's experience, Watkins had very transactional relationships. He was a user. 'Generally speaking, he'd have been friends with somebody that got value from being friends with him for whatever reason it might be.'

* * *

Legend has it that the British slang word for paedophile, 'nonce', may actually have originated in Wakefield. The story goes that it comes from an acronym used by staff there. N.O.N.C.E. stood for 'not on normal courtyard exercise' and would be marked on the cell card of any prisoner (like Ian Watkins or Roy Whiting) who may be in danger of violence from other prisoners so that staff would not open their doors whilst other prisoners were out. This story was corroborated by our contributor Pete.

The claim received widespread currency after it was made, and grabbed our attention, on a highly popular 2022 Channel 5 documentary, *HMP Wakefield: Evil Behind Bars*. However, according to the *Oxford English Dictionary (OED)*, 'nonce' may be a derivative from the word 'nance', a derogatory term for an effeminate or gay man, or may derive from a Lincolnshire dialect word, 'nonse', meaning 'good for nothing'. That said, the *OED* does qualify this by stating that 'nonce' is of unknown origin, with the earliest known use of the word only coming in the 1970s. *OED*'s earliest evidence for 'nonce' is from 1970, in the writing of historian Tony Parker.

Perhaps it's just because we like the Wakefield origin story, but it seems a little odd that if the word has ancient origins it would only emerge in print in the 1970s. We are true-crime writers not etymologists though; we will leave others to draw their own conclusions!

* * *

Roy Whiting is currently serving time at Wakefield after he was found guilty of the abduction and murder of eight-year-old Sarah Payne. Sarah lived in Hersham, Surrey and was playing with her siblings in a cornfield near their grandparents' house in Ferring, near Worthing, when she disappeared. Her body was found a fortnight later in undergrowth off the A29 road, fifteen miles away from where she had disappeared.

Her extraordinary mother, Sara Payne, became a campaigner in the wake of this unimaginably appalling thing happening to her little girl. In 2011, 'Sarah's Law' was passed in England and Wales, which allows anyone to find out whether a person who has contact with children is a child sex offender. It emerged that before he murdered Sarah, Whiting had been incarcerated for the kidnap and indecent assault of a nine-year-old girl in 1995. He was imprisoned for a minimum of fifty years in 2001, although in 2010 it was reduced by ten years by the High Court.

Because he is a child murderer and sex offender, he is the lowest of the low, even in Monster Mansion. Since being there, he has been attacked multiple times by fellow inmates. In 2002 he was attacked with a razor and left with a six-inch scar on his right cheek; in 2011 he was stabbed in the eye; and in 2018 he was stabbed by two other inmates in his cell and had to be taken to hospital.

Our prison contact is convinced that Whiting is doomed in prison.

I've seen him get attacked twice, once by this Ricky, and Gary Vinter who I met [a Muslim]. Whiting is on D wing. He never comes out of his cell. He just chain smokes. He wears prison clothing, he is like a tramp. He works in workshop 8 using a sewing machine. He goes to work, comes back and stays in his cell. If an inmate wants a move from HMP W they just attack him. Recently the media has reported Whiting has been attacked again. In my opinion, and that of many in here, it is just a matter of time before he is murdered. He can't keep surviving these attacks. Surely one will be fatal.

The recent attack the prisoner mentions came towards the end of writing this book; on 13 February 2024 it was reported that Whiting had been attacked again. Aged fifty-nine years old by this point, he was taken from Wakefield prison to hospital with stab wounds. Later declared to be stable, he was returned to the prison.

At the time of writing, paedophile Mark Bridger is still in there as well. He abducted and murdered five-year-old April Jones in 2012, a crime, like the murder of Sarah Payne, that shocked the whole nation. On 30 May 2013, he was found guilty of April's abduction and murder, as well as perverting the course of justice. He was sentenced to life imprisonment with a whole-life tariff, which as we know is both a rare sentence, reserved for the most heinous crimes, and means he will never be released. Like many of these lowest of the low, he has been attacked in Wakefield, as we described in our Prologue.

The Vulnerable Prisoner Unit (VPU), or as inmates often term it, the 'beast wing', is used to house the likes of Watkins, Whiting and Bridger, individuals who are at real risk of a violent, possibly lethal attack if amongst the mainstream prison population. A compelling report into VPUs by the prison and probation service suggested that the legendary hierarchy that places nonces at the bottom, the baddest of the bad, in the prisoners' pile, is very much the case. It also suggests that this hierarchy breaks down into even further layers, and that the younger the victims of the paedophile are – babies in Watkins' case – the lower in this hierarchy of horror they sit.

There is a quandary for these individuals. At the bottom of the prison hierarchy, they are likely to be brutally attacked on the main prison wings. However, on the VPU, particularly for younger offenders, there is the real risk of sexual assault from the older, established paedophile sex offenders.

* * *

Martin recalled one Cat A prisoner.

> *Every time he had a picture taken of him, he would smile and when asked why would say, 'I don't want people seeing my photo and thinking I'm a bad man'. He was doing twenty-five years for murder. These people care what people think of them more than we may know. People with a big reputation maybe didn't have to look over their shoulders as much at Wakefield. Sex offenders were common and everything was so regimented that the prisoners were used to it.*

Crimes as sickening as those alluded to in this chapter are distressing for us even to write about, as parents ourselves and as human beings. They have been covered extensively elsewhere too. What we did want to know, and say, more about was how these prisoners interact with other prisoners and what the staff make of them. The answers often surprised us.

Jo Taylor has no time for any of the nonces but was particularly disgusted by her interactions with the child molester and serial killer Sidney Cooke, who raped and murdered Mark Tildesley, Jason Swift and Barry Lewis.

'Paedophiles are so slimy.' She mimics them in a high ingratiating voice: "Hi, Miss." Daniel Lomas was slimy. He got out. Sidney Cooke was old even when I was there. Disgusting. He was part of the Wolf Pack. There was a book written all about Sidney Cooke and the Wolf Pack.'

Sidney Cooke made a bid for parole that was rejected in May 2023 when he was ninety-six years old, as they considered him to *still* be a danger to the public. Whether this is the case or not, given the horrific nature of his crimes there can be few individuals more deserving of dying inside the high walls of Wakefield.

Although disgusted by her proximity to individuals such as Cooke, Jo was emphatic that she didn't feel personally threatened.

'The nonces were no problem for us because they are not violent to adults.'

'Never trust anyone' is Jo's thinking after Wakefield. She came from Wetherby and 'they were bad lads – murders etc. – but there was very little protection. Fuck. These look like normal people! You wouldn't know they were murderers or rapists. Always go with your gut feeling. I can pick a nonce out.'

Our contributor Vanessa, on the other hand, was very

traumatised by some of her interactions with the sex offenders. We asked her if she met or interacted with any of the prisoners she had mentioned to us, who had crossed over between Wormwood Scrubs and Wakefield.

Whilst she confirmed that she did not interact with any of the prisoners who crossed over between the two prisons, she observed that when Brixton Prison closed down, they did have to integrate sex offenders with the other prisoners, which was very difficult. The other prisoners knew they were sex offenders.

'Usually, lifers just want to get on with it and don't have many issues but having an influx of lots of sex offenders upset things and was very difficult, and there were lots of issues.'

We were keen to get her take on what kind of issues she was talking about. She explained that the prisoners would say, 'Can't you get shot of them, Gov? What are these nonces doing on our wing?'

It was a very trying time for Vanessa to attempt to keep everybody safe and secure.

'When you have issues like that it is unnerving, when there is something that can rock the boat so easily; it is also difficult to get the staff on board in times like that because some of them [the prisoners] have done horrendous crimes.'

Everything Vanessa said reiterated the information we were getting from our research and other contributors. Sex offenders are a different and difficult type of prisoner; paedophile sex offenders and child murderers are even worse, and they are viewed with contempt and disgust by many other more 'mainstream' category A offenders. She had a powerful way of putting this.

'If somebody has young kids and somebody comes along who's just murdered two little kids, it is a very difficult path to walk. The higher up you go, the more diplomatic you have to be, and lead by example to both staff and prisoners.'

In Vanessa's view you have to be consciously aware of how you treat those kinds of prisoners, because the crimes that they commit separate them. This is obviously an emotive and triggering experience for inmates, but it must be for staff as well.

'You never get any training to work with sex offenders, unless you go to a specialist jail like Grendon, which is all full of sex offenders.'

HMP Grendon is Britain's only specialist therapeutic prison for the treatment of sex offenders. However, it's not the norm. While at a prison like Grendon, staff receive CBT training and specialist help, that has not been Vanessa's experience in her career. 'In normal Cat B, Cat A jails, you don't get training to deal with sexual offences or horrific murders or serial killers or anything like that.'

As we will see later in the book, at times this left her feeling traumatised and vulnerable. It's hard to believe that there is not extensive training to prepare all staff to cope with working with paedophiles and sex offenders.

Vanessa also raises the lack of training for dealing with serial killers. We can only conclude that even officers dealing with the former Wakefield inhabitant who may have killed more people than any other, Harold Shipman, had no form of training that could properly prepare them.

If any training could.

Chapter 10

Harold Shipman

While we were keen to focus on current and recent inmates of Wakefield in telling our story, no book about Wakefield would be complete without a chapter on Harold Shipman. In the face of stiff competition from the monsters, past and present, who have walked into Wakefield's cells, Shipman is widely believed to be the most prolific serial killer in modern history. He has been nicknamed 'Dr Death' and 'The Angel of Death'.

Born Harold Frederick Shipman on 14 January 1946 and known as Fred Shipman to acquaintances, it was his position of authority and trust as a GP that allowed him to carry out his murder spree.

We will probably never know the final, grim tally of the deaths at his hands, but it has been estimated at 250 victims. On 31 January 2000 Shipman was found guilty of the murder of fifteen of his patients, and was sentenced to life imprisonment with a whole-life order. On 13 January 2004, he hanged himself in his cell at Wakefield, the day before what would have been his fifty-eighth birthday.

He had been on suicide watch at his two previous prisons, but controversially it was deemed not necessary for him to continue on the 'special measure' of suicide watch when he was transferred to Wakefield. We explore this in more detail shortly, in our chapter dedicated to this practice, which clearly broke down catastrophically on this occasion.

Shipman's targets were vulnerable elderly people, overwhelmingly women, who he killed with an abnormal amount, or fatal dose, of drugs. It is mercifully rare for a British medical professional to be found guilty of murdering patients in their care, although there are chilling echoes in far more recent cases.

Shipman graduated with a medicine degree from the Leeds School of Medicine, University of Leeds in 1970, and started his working life at Pontefract General Infirmary in the West Riding of Yorkshire. His first GP position came in 1974 at the Abraham Ormerod Medical Centre. His first brush with the law came when he was caught forging pethidine prescriptions for his own use. After paying a £600 fine followed by a short stint at a drug rehabilitation centre in York, he worked as a GP in Manchester for many years, establishing his own practice at 21 Market Street in 1993.

By a bizarre coincidence, Shipman was the GP of one of our contributor's grandmothers: Lisa. They were both from the same area and so she knew of him before he went to prison.

'He was actually my grandmother's GP. He was quite good. Well, he was great for my grandma! My grandma to be honest was one of the lucky ones!'

Once he was banged up in Wakefield, Lisa said, 'I'd met him [before] but he didn't recognise me.'

'In the prison he very much kept himself to himself, and rarely interacted with staff. He didn't want to interact with staff, he felt he was superior.' He would spend his time watching TV and reading books. The only times he came out of his cell were meal times. He didn't come out very much, Lisa reckoned, because he was so notorious, he might have been scared to leave his door open in case someone was to come in and assault him.

Going back to his eventual arrest, the first whistle-blower was Dr Linda Reynolds of the Brooke Surgery in Hyde, who flagged concerns about the high death rate of Shipman's patients to the local coroner in March 1998. She thought the large number of cremations for elderly women that he asked to have counter-signed was dodgy, but police found insufficient evidence and closed the investigation. Way down the line, one of many findings of the two-year-long Shipman Inquiry into all the deaths certified by Shipman was that Greater Manchester Police had put inexperienced officers on the case.

Shipman was at liberty to kill three more people. John Shaw, a taxi driver, then came forward to the police. He suspected Shipman of murdering twenty-one elderly fares he had taken to hospital, apparently in good health until they came under Shipman's care. Kathleen Grundy, former Mayor of Hyde, was found dead at home on 24 June 1998: Shipman was the last person to see her alive and signed her death certificate, recording that she died of 'old age'. Exposed when her will revealed that she had excluded her family but left £386,000 to Shipman, Grundy's body was exhumed and showed traces of heroin. Shipman claimed that she was a heroin addict but when he tried to use his own medical journal as evidence to back his claim, it became clear he had entered those notes on his computer after her death.

He was arrested on 7 September 1998. Investigation into a test sample of other suspicious deaths revealed that a lethal dose of heroin was his favoured modus operandi, along with signing the death certificates and falsifying medical records. Commencing on 5 October 1999 at Preston Crown Court, Shipman's trial saw him charged with the murder of fifteen women by lethal injection of diamorphine between 1995 and 1998. On the last day of January 2000, the jury found him guilty of fifteen counts of murder and also one count of forgery, as police had discovered the typewriter that he used to forge Kathleen Grundy's will.

Mr Justice Forbes sentenced him to life imprisonment with a recommendation that he serve a whole-life tariff. Authorities were aware that plenty more charges could have been brought. Given that he already had fifteen life sentences, though, there was no need. Shipman himself always denied his guilt, never made any public statements about his actions, and continued to be supported by his wife Primrose after his conviction, who maintained his innocence.

During his doomed stint at Wakefield, his refusal to participate in courses which would have encouraged acknowledgement of his crimes led to him having privileges temporarily suspected, including the chance to ring his wife.

Our contributor Pete left Wakefield in 2000, so Shipman came after his time, but he knew the officer who found him dead. 'Sam Shoemaker' was his nickname. As Pete explained, 'He [Shipman] killed himself because if he reached sixty-five years old his wife wouldn't have gotten his pension. Didn't tell anybody but he just did it... His death was hush-hush: a secret cremation.'

Martin Baker, however, *was* working at Wakefield when Shipman committed suicide. One of the main places that Martin would interact with prisoners was the gym, and Shipman did not really go there. However, hilariously, his new 'patients' often did.

'When I was dealing with people down the gym and they were coming in with remedials, I'd say. "Oh yeah you might have a slight ligament tear there or something." They would reply, "Oh well, Harold Shipman says I've got a so-and-so!" and I'd say, "Well, he can't treat you anyway so I don't care what he says you've got!"'

Then people would be put on remedials by the doctors and sent to see Martin.

'And they would come in fully knowing – or think they're knowing – what they've got, and nine times out of ten they didn't have anything near what they thought they had!'

As an aside, our contributor Pete had offered us some, admittedly speculative, information about how he witnessed prisoners being medicated that might offer further context for why they were keen to use Shipman as their informal in-house GP.

They used to give what they called the 'nutters medication'. Bloody hell, it used to knock them flipping out! The doctor would come down and flipping inject them, Christ knows what the hell they were injecting them with. But they'd just flipping go all bloody loose! But we just did as we were told, we didn't have a bloody clue what the doctor were giving them. But it quietened them down. We'd hold them while the doctor gave them a bloody injection, and that's how they dealt with mental health. Barbaric!

Pete also described the use of placebos – 'It just shut them up, because they'd asked for medication' – as a common practice.

A lot of them were given chalk. They would say they'd got a headache, and they were forever having loads of medication. You know the round pieces of chalk? We used to cut them into tablet form, and you'd say, 'There you go kid, couple of them. There were three little pots, there were a dark, a medium and a light. So, if they went up and said they had a sore throat – 'get some of that dark'; if they went up and said they had headache – 'get one of them light'.

Pete claims to have tried this remedy himself for a sore throat: it was 'quite good for soothing your throat'. Staff couldn't afford to take time off sick or any time to see a doctor.

Returning to Shipman's story though, Martin said that, like any other prisoner, if you suspected they were a threat to themselves you would put them on watch. Especially a well-known or high-risk prisoner. However, they know how to meet the criteria in order to get taken off the watch, and you cannot keep every prisoner on suicide watch at all times. You have to trust, and with Shipman he explained:

He knew exactly what he was doing, he knew exactly when the staff were going to check him, he knew exactly at what time in the morning the staff were going to count. The night staff had to do a count, at 5, 5.30, they have to do a count and they start either on the fours or ones, depending if you wanted to go up first or down first. So, once he'd been checked, he knew he wasn't going to be checked for another ten–fifteen minutes; that's enough time to die, and that's when he did it.

That was his window.

Though he preceded her employment, Jo Taylor had certainly been privy to conversations about his suicide when she served as an officer at Wakefield.

'Shipman was there [and spent time in the segregation unit] before my time. They had brought him off the watch. Shipman got elderly women to change their wills...'

Jo corroborated that Shipman knew exactly what he was doing, and why.

'He only killed himself because of some date that if he died, she got the pension. He'd been taken off suicide watch.'

We said we thought that was weird.

Not if he knew what he was doing and continually showed there's not [a cause for concern]... You don't just have an SO. In his case there would have been a governor there. Not the number one governor, but you would have a governor, SO, chaplaincy and probation: all these people discussing everything before taking him off the watch! When the cons couldn't get what they wanted they used to be queuing up outside his cell, apparently. He'd been treating them! Can't have been medication, just advice. Flipping monster. He killed hundreds.

Martin went on to tell us that Shipman had said that when everything was sorted out, and he was happy and his solicitor was happy that she'd [Shipman's wife] get insurance money and things, and everything was in position, he could then commit suicide, and he did.

No one would have known that he had everything in place. He wouldn't have told the staff that.

Furthermore, Martin said that prisoners often say they are going to kill themselves.

'Everybody has bad days, all prisoners don't like being in prison and some use it as an excuse: "I'm going to kill myself, oh quick we'll open a hatch." They like the attention.'

You have experts within the prison who will assess the prisoner, and if they're not considered a risk then they weren't a risk. Martin smiled.

Shipman wasn't a problem. He was a model prisoner really. Prisoners went to him for advice, medical matters. Of course, it was an annoyance to the medical officer, because he [Shipman] might say, 'Oh yeah, you need to be on tramadol' and they all wanted to be on tramadol because it's the type of drug it is. Whereas the doctor might say, 'I'm going to give you liquid paracetamol.' 'Well I don't want paracetamol, Shipman said I should be on…' 'No no no.' It was easy for people to go into his cell and say, 'Oh I've got this wrong with me', because that's what he'd done all his life. It was easy for him to offer advice, but of course nobody had to comply with that advice because he was no longer a practising GP, he had no power.

We asked whether he was a popular prisoner. 'People didn't really have a problem with him. What he'd done was not a very nice crime but people were in there for far worse crimes than him. It was just that he was so high profile.'

Shipman had used his bed sheets to hang himself from the window bars of his cell, and was pronounced dead at 08.10 after hanging himself at 06.20 that fateful day in mid-January 2004. He had apparently told his probation officer that he was pondering suicide in order to ensure that his wife received a full NHS pension, which she would not have been entitled to if he lived beyond sixty, given that he was stripped of his pension, and struck off the GMC register, following his conviction.

This incident had a lasting impact at Wakefield. Lisa's colleague was the one to find him after he committed suicide.

'Sad to say it really affected him.'

Lisa has no idea why Shipman was taken off suicide watch. Her husband Paul told us that protocols for checking prisoners came into effect after his suicide. It used to be that on nights Cat A prisoners were checked every hour, but it changed to five times an hour after his death.

The Shipman Inquiry's first report, published in July 2002, concluded that he had killed at least 218 of his patients between 1975 and 1998. A follow-up report issued in late January 2005, alleged that Shipman had killed three patients, and stated serious suspicions about four further deaths, including a four-year-old girl, during his early career at Pontefract General Infirmary. 459 people died while under his care between 1971 and 1998, but as he was often the only doctor to certify a death, it will never be known how many of them were murder victims; the educated guesstimate is 250... A grim record we can only hope will never be 'beaten' by another serial killer.

Another very notorious prisoner had tried and failed to commit suicide, albeit not at Wakefield. We can hope it was a sense of remorse at his terrible crimes that drove Ian Huntley to make the attempt. We also know, however, that many prisoners at every prison he has been held in have been keen to make his prison time a living hell, and maybe that was what drove him to the attempt on his own life.

Chapter II

Ian Huntley

Ian Huntley was born on 31 January 1974 in Grimsby, Lincolnshire. While working as a school caretaker in Soham, Cambridgeshire, in August 2002, he abducted and murdered two ten-year-old schoolfriends, Holly Wells and Jessica Chapman. The girls' bodies were discovered in a ditch in Suffolk on 17 August 2002. On 4 August, Huntley, who was the caretaker at the local secondary school, Soham Village College, apparently lured the girls into his house by claiming that his girlfriend, Maxine Carr, who was the two girls' year five teaching assistant at St Andrews Primary School, was also at home, whereas in fact she was visiting her mother in Grimsby.

Ian Huntley had a long history of violence and sexual assault, targeting women and children between 1992 and 2002 without ever being brought to justice. He used the alias Ian Nixon when he successfully applied for the senior caretaker position at the college, and no background checks were conducted on him.

Soon after his sentencing, Huntley stated of the decades in prison ahead of him: 'I'll rot in here, I know it. I'll spend the rest of my life in here… I'm going to be inside forever and it'll be torture.'

This self-pitying tone is all too familiar to our contributors who spent time with him.

Lisa spent three nights watching him during her night shifts. 'He didn't really want to interact with staff. And I found him quite pitiful. Feeling sorry for himself, "woe is me", that kind of thing.'

He was on a constant watch. He was supervised twenty-four hours a day in the care centre when he first came to Wakefield. 'All he did was read newspapers. At that initial time, that's all he did,' she added.

In our contributor Paul's opinion: 'His profile was such that the Shipman incident carried over to him, so that when he came to Wakefield, because of what happened with Shipman, everybody was terrified that he was gonna kill himself, and that couldn't happen.'

Therefore, he was put on a 24/7 watch: 'A lot of money was spent making sure that he didn't kill himself.' Huntley wasn't beyond manipulating this persona, either. 'He was quite a needy individual. He played on the fact that he knew that nothing could happen to him… He threatened to kill himself on a regular basis.'

Still, it's not paranoia if they're really out to get you, as the saying goes. Huntley has been a very prized scalp inside

Wakefield, the combination of the utterly shocking nature of the Soham murders and his notoriety ensuring he has been right in the firing line for other cons to go for him. On 14 September 2005 in Wakefield, he was badly burned when Mark Hobson threw boiling water over him. He was subsequently too badly injured to attend the hearing a fortnight later where they determined what his minimum term of imprisonment was going to be – 40 years.

Huntley launched a £15,000 compensation claim after this incident, alleging that the HMP Wakefield authorities had failed in their duty of care towards him, and apparently with the support of £2,500 in legal aid.

Huntley left Wakefield in late January 2008 for Frankland. There, he was attacked again when his throat was slashed by the armed robber Damien Fowkes. He was hospitalised and made another compensation claim, for £20,000 in damages.

Martin was PO on nights when Huntley took an overdose and they had to send him out of the hospital. 'He saved up his tablets.'

Martin phoned the hospital and an ambulance: 'You've got a prisoner coming in.' 'Who is it?' 'I'm afraid I can't say.' 'What do you mean you can't say?' 'You cannot know his name. You're not allowed to know his name.' Because he was high profile.

Martin had to send most of his staff out to take him to hospital because of how well Huntley was known, whilst himself and one other officer had to manage the rest of the prison. He couldn't use seg or hospital staff, so it was just the two of them. Around 650 prisoners between two people (excluding prisoners in seg or hospital). If something else had gone wrong they wouldn't have been able to cope. Martin found the duty governor and he didn't seem bothered. The ECR (emergency control room) couldn't find anyone to help step up. The duty governor was then told off as he could have gone in to help and he didn't.

'If something else had gone wrong, that was it. We were snookered.'

Martin, another gate officer and one more had to run the nights operations by themselves. Suicide checks, checking on Cat As. At certain times they had to hit a switch on the wall, called 'pegging', to say you had been round to check the prisoners.

Whilst in the hospital, someone took a picture of Huntley and the next day he was in the press. He hadn't managed to do the deed though.

'Even though it rendered him unconscious, the medication wouldn't have killed him. He would have had to have been found very, very late, two or three days; he was never gonna be in that position. So as soon as he was found on the floor unconscious, the hospital officers went straight in.'

Martin described Ian Huntley to us in contemptuous terms.

'He's another pathetic individual. I can't say anything nice about him because there was nothing nice. He was just very needy, always on suicide watch.'

Huntley had someone at his door twenty-four hours per

day and was never on normal location. It was expensive. 'The cost of looking after him was astronomical really,' Martin added, then paused to sum up Huntley.

'He was such a wet lettuce leaf.'

When faced with a horrific criminal like Huntley, Pete told us that you have to put everything they've done to the back of your mind, because they'll one day ask for something like a new toilet roll and 'You can't say, "No, F Off," you have to give them what they're entitled to. And that's difficult.'

Pete then added that 'the prisoners cringe when they see themselves on TV. Wakefield is full of sex criminals so they're always on the news.'

Huntley, he cringes. When he were at Wakefield [Dave Thompson, Governor at the time] was told that if Ian Huntley committed suicide at Wakefield, he would lose his job. He was so much in the public eye, it would be a huge public spectacle if he died. These are the types of people we worked with; absolutely horrendous. But when you go in there, put that uniform on, you've got to be professional... When the shit hit the fan, they flipping got on with it and they made it work.

Jo had first-hand Huntley stories, too.

He was there when I joined. He was on the hospital wing. He was on a constant watch. You've got your constant watches, which is an officer there all the time.

In New Hall you had fifteen-minute watches. When I got to Wakefield, I was like 'How many on fifteen-minute watch?' 'No.' 'Half hour?' 'No.' 'An hour?' I left New Hall and the wing I was on had seventeen on suicide watches. There was one on five obs an hour. Others were on fifteen minutes, a half hour. When I got to Wakefield, there were only three on watch.

So why was Huntley singled out for suicide watch if it was not the norm?

When he was on normal observation he got attacked, so they put him in the hospital wing on constant watch. I did overtime once with him. I only did overtime twice at Wakefield. I didn't mind at New Hall: you would do mother and baby – I didn't mind that – big chairs, private room, picnic. I did one with Huntley, he was on the healthcare, he says, 'Are you new?' I said, yes, I was a new SO at Wakefield. He asked where I was from, I said New Hall.

He sneered, 'Oh, she was in there.' I said 'Who?' He was on about Maxine Carr. I said, 'No, she was at Foston Hall [a prison in Derbyshire]. It was her mother who was at New Hall for perverting the course of justice!' He went, 'Oh yeah', carrying on. I had to follow him round.

We will come to the Braille work done by the prisoners later in our story, but it was very interesting to learn that Huntley was one of those who learned this highly trained skill.

'He had a job transcribing books from normal writing into Braille. I sat and watched him for twelve hours,' Jo told us.

This level of vigilance turned out to be warranted. On 5 September 2006, in HMP Frankland, Huntley attempted to kill himself with an overdose of anti-depressants he had been hoarding in his cell. He did not succeed, though, and the attempt resulted only in another hospitalisation.

Huntley has made three failed suicide attempts to date.

Chapter 12

Suicide Watch

Wakefield has, unfortunately, had its share of suicides over the years, most notoriously Harold Shipman. Lisa described some more detail around the procedure for us, which in her view tends to be poorly understood.

There's different levels of suicide watch is what a lot of people don't fully understand. Ian Huntley is a prime example. He was on a twenty-four-hour one, so he was on what we call constant watch. Where some prisoners can be on one every fifteen minutes, so you just go and check them every fifteen minutes and make sure they're okay. But it's during that fifteen minutes that something can happen and it's usually just out of your control. What people have to bear in mind is there's only x amount of staff to quite a lot of prisoners. And what they do to prevent suicide is massive. People don't see that. They don't see the amount of work that goes into preventing it in the first place.

For our contributor John, even in a job that could be as tough as his, managing death was one of the hardest things that he had to deal with. He has been in the position where he has had to speak to families of the deceased and explain that their family members were dead. On the other side of it, he has also successfully navigated people out of suicidal thoughts.

He recalled to us that some prisoners were so intent on suicide that they would have to be kept in a cell with a transparent door with an officer at the door watching 24/7, sometimes for months on end. As he puts it: 'It's about routinely ensuring that there's a presence there, and that somebody is concerned about their welfare.'

John described it as marvellous to be able to support people, and there are many things staff can do to support prisoners, but it's only possible if you are aware that there is a problem. If a prisoner is not open to help and accepting support, there is not much to be done.

Reflecting on his experiences discussing prisoner welfare outside of work, John notes that many people don't tend to have empathy for such high-level criminals.

'If you mention that [your job is dealing with suicidal class A prisoners] in the pub, some smart arse is going to say, "They're better off dead aren't they? Let them get on with it!" So, my experience is you don't talk about that out there.'

John explained that this is why peer relationships with fellow officers are so key. Only your peers truly understand the responsibilities and expectations of working in a prison. 'We accept that it's a life, it's your duty to do that.'

In Vanessa's case, as a former prison governor, she claims to have lost cost count of how many suicides she was directly involved in or had to deal with. You can even become desensitised to death in such great numbers. 'I used to think, well there must be something wrong with me because why aren't I batting an eyelid when something like that happens…'

Her coping mechanism was to direct her focus onto maintaining the regime and looking after the other prisoners by keeping it all very in the moment; she managed her response by trying not to look back.

We were curious to know more about the process. What happens when the body of a Harold Shipman is discovered? Whatever the high-security prison, the basic protocols are the same, and Vanessa was highly well-placed to tell us more.

She described that early steps include phoning the coroner, and making sure that the staff who found the dead body are okay. It is also crucial that any prisoners involved – friends of the deceased or bunkmates, or if it was a prisoner that found the body – are okay, too.

You have then got to have a debrief with staff, and make sure everybody has written statements. It may appear at this point that you are only interested in the staff reports as opposed to staff wellbeing, but Vanessa emphasised that actually such documentation is very, very important and should be completed asap. 'In a coroners' court your statement may be used and cross examined six to eight months later [and that] can lead to even bigger issues down the line.'

The room of death is sealed off. The police are called and access to the room is controlled. The death is reported to the duty governor, the area manager: all the higher-ups. There is a very methodical checklist, Vanessa went on:

'In suicides particularly, there's nothing you can do. The person is dead. But there is an awful lot that you have to do. You have to go into overdrive to make sure everything's been completed. You never really have time for you – it's all about everybody else. That is a shortfall of the prison service. The higher up you go it's like you're invincible, and you're really not.'

In such a stressful situation, where your position of high responsibility necessitates so much complex administrative work, and role-modelling to more junior staff, it must be tempting to bury yourself in the mandatory activities, and bury your feelings along with it. Vanessa seemed to concur.

'I can remember my first, and I can remember my last, any of the others in between I can't remember.'

We were curious to know how someone like Harold Shipman managed to kill himself.

'Quite often there are no signs and sometimes there is nothing you can do to help,' Vanessa told us.

Prisons are under-resourced. In Vanessa's case, with over 300 prisoners and just six staff, it was impossible to monitor everyone at all times. She gave the hypothetical example of someone who could be on an 'every fifteen-minutes observation' suicide watch: 'But it's their cell mate who's not on any type of watch that might need the support. Just because you're suicidal doesn't mean you're going to tell people.'

For all these reasons, you can end up with the bitterly ironic scenario at Wakefield of Robert Maudsley begging to be allowed to commit suicide and therefore being denied the opportunity, whilst Harold Shipman, who as a serial killer doctor was uniquely well-placed to think of creative and efficient ways to dispatch himself, was taken off the suicide watch.

* * *

Of course, not every prison death is a suicide, and with resourcing stretched, it can also be difficult to go by the book on every occasion with these incidents too. They always cause a ripple of anxiety amongst the other inmates, and we received a first-hand prisoner account of the peculiar demise of Trevor Hardy.

'Trevor Hardy the Manchester beast. A very high-profile serial killing case in the 1980s. Hardy, a tiny little bald-headed man, was very well dressed. He was a loner in prison. He worked with [Roy] Whiting in workshop 8. The sewing machine shop.'

Born on 11 June 1945, Trevor Hardy, known as the 'Beast of Manchester', as our prisoner also notes, was a notorious serial killer of young girls in the Manchester area between December 1974 and March 1976. His first victim was fifteen-year-old Janet Lesley Stewart, who he stabbed to death on New Year's Eve 1974. His next teenage female victim was seventeen-year-old Wanda Skala, who he murdered on 19 July 1975. Then, in March 1976, he murdered Sharon Mosoph, also seventeen years old. He had stripped and mutilated Wanda and Sharon's bodies.

After a huge manhunt, he was apprehended in August 1976 and sentenced to three life sentences, one for each murder, with a minimum of thirty years, at Manchester Crown Court on 2 May 1978. This was time that he would serve at Wakefield until his death decades later. He collapsed in Wakefield on 23 September 2012 and died two days later in hospital aged sixty-seven. The grisly manner of his death in custody, however, was memorably recounted to us by a prisoner who claims to have witnessed it.

I was there when he died. He was located on C wing, the twos near the servery. Staff claimed he was found dead in bed on the Saturday morning. Indeed, staff entered his cell, a nurse came and all concluded he was dead, this was at 9am. As with prison deaths in cells, the body was covered up, his cell door was locked, the observation access on the door was taped up to stop inmates looking in at the dead body. Later the undertaker would come and take the body at night when we was all locked up. His body was left there. At 11.45am we was in a line outside his door waiting for dinner to be served at the servery. Staff [security] returned to the cell to take photos. They entered the cell. They discovered him alive, he was groaning, the alarm was raised and an ambulance was called. Hardy was taken to hospital. It was confirmed he had had a stroke. He did die days later but they left him all morning believing he was dead. The ombudsman wanted to interview prisoners, but they never did speak to any offenders.

Pete talked to us about the impact of prisoner deaths on staff as well as other inmates.

Any death is horrendous. Especially in custody. It's a community is a prison. It's got everything you'd get on the outside with the exception of a pub. You've got the canteen, you've got the home, because the cells are their home. A lot of long-term prisoners take a great deal of pride in their cells because it's where they spend most of their time. So, it does impact a hell of a lot. The suicides in prison have just risen massively over the last twenty years.

When you suspect someone's at risk of suicide, they are put on ACCT surveillance. ACCT stands for Assessment, Care in Custody and Teamwork, and it is the care planning process for prisoners who are deemed at risk of serious self-harm. It doesn't always prevent tragedy, and some of the recollections still hurt Pete.

Remember a lad who was doing a natural life sentence. He had a parole hearing, second/third hearing. He got rejected for parole and committed suicide because he couldn't see a way out of jail. And he were a smashing lad, and I remember him saying to the staff the night before, 'See you tomorrow Mr so-and-so.' In prison you were 'boss' or 'mister', they didn't call you Pete. 'See you tomorrow boss' – but he never did. He took his own life.

After a death you have to put up a notice to staff and a notice to prisoners informing them. Deaths in custody are always investigated, rightly so, as they might have to be treated as a murder scene. Police are called immediately and they view it as a possible crime scene. Everyone's goings-in-and-out of the cell must be recorded, and samples are taken from the cell. If you go into the cell, you may have your fingerprints taken so you can be eliminated from the enquiries. They do the same things they'd do outside of prison upon finding a death.

Lisa was also eloquent on the impact of prison death.

It affects both staff and prisoners. If it's a suicide it's really bad. You have an understanding, and death can cause people to come together in a strangely morbid way. When you have to talk to the friends of the deceased, you talk it out. Even though we know what that prisoner was in for and it's not very nice, they were still a human being and still somebody's son, somebody's brother, somebody's dad.

Perhaps the most famous prison suicide was that of Fred West, which drove the tabloids into a frenzy about the husband and wife serial killer couple all over again, not least because his suicide note was a macabre love letter to his wife. It's time for us to share the testimony we have received about the UK's most famous living female prisoner, Rose West.

Chapter 13

Rose West

As we described at the start of the book in our history of HMP Wakefield, HMP New Hall is essentially Wakefield's female prison. Its notorious inmates include Rosemary (Rose) West. New Hall started out in 1933 as a 'halfway house' for prisoners at Wakefield coming towards the end of their sentence. The two prisons have maintained very close links since then, and many of the prison officers that we spoke to have spent time at both establishments.

New Hall can accommodate up to 381 women, although it is not always at capacity, as its 2022 Inspection Report revealed. At the time of that inspection, New Hall only housed 314 women. That report praised the management of Governor Julia Spence, saying that the prison was 'well-led'. The prison has a first-night centre for new arrivals, a mother and baby unit, three main wings and a segregation unit. Most cells are not ensuite but there are thirty ensuite rooms for women who, for example, are deemed to have special needs because of personality disorders.

In terms of leisure activities for the women, there is yoga, a drama class, film nights and an excellent gym. Cookery classes are also available, and according to press reports Rose West had utilised this facility in order to become an excellent baker. The Zumba classes we have read about may be a more recent addition.

Jo Taylor recalled that:

> *Rosemary West is in New Hall prison now. I saw that Rose West changed her name to Jennifer Jones in Durham. I saw her pet bird in her cell there but not her. I think it was Durham Prison where I saw Rose West, because that had men and women. More like two sections, not like one. I only went up there once. We dropped off a prisoner. We were on the wings and that. They were saying, 'I will show you Rose West's call. She wasn't there. She was probably in education. It was because of the budgie. Lifers in those days were entitled to budgies. They would have a budgie as a pet. I don't think they have that anymore. This was the late 1990s. I would have liked to have seen Rose West. It was just a regular cell.*

Having worked at both prisons, Jo is always drawing interesting comparisons.

In Wakefield, there just seemed to be more in the men's cells – like stereo systems. In New Hall they tended to just have a radio cassette or something. When I was at New Hall they used to be able to have clothes sent in and I think they stopped that, because of drugs paraphernalia. Back in the day they could order stuff from Argos. Women could order make-up.

Not every cell has a pet bird, but they do have plenty in common. Each individual cell at New Hall is pretty cramped: about three metres long and 1.8 metres wide. Spending at least twenty-two hours within this space, the women have limited interaction with the world outside their cell. They might speak to a cleaner or two, their key worker in prison and prison officers. Plenty of this contact will be conducted through the hatch in their cell door.

Each cell is kitted out in the same basic way. In addition to a single bed, toilet and chair, there is a storage unit. Prisoners can watch TV, and read books and newspapers. They are allowed an hour a day of exercise outside in the prison grounds. As we have seen, police vet prison visits very intensively, and a prisoner is usually allowed only around one hour-long visit a fortnight.

Handwritten letters, both sent and received, are perhaps the most significant form of contact with the outside world, but there is very little privacy as the contents of most of them are checked by prison staff. Ditto emails, which are printed out, again, checked, and delivered by prison officers. The prisoner is charged 40p for each email received through the Email a Prisoner service. Phone calls can only be received from people on the women's friends and family list.

Jo Taylor featured on *Jailbirds*, a TV show made about New Hall while she was working there. She described the prison's setting to us.

'Flockton [the village] is just around the corner of the train station. You can get promoted from New Hall to Wakefield and vice versa. You get male staff in New Hall that hide behind women.'

Jo let us in on another striking and, to us, surprising contrast, too: 'Wakefield doesn't smell. The women's cells in New Hall stank, especially on the drug wing.'

In his Inspection Report published in January 2023, Charlie Taylor, HM Chief Inspector of Prisons, was broadly positive but did not make New Hall sound as cushy as the tabloid stories about West's life behind bars might suggest.

The prison was very well led by a governor who knew her prison well and was able to motivate an engaged and caring staff group. This was true of all elements of the prison, including various specialist facilities such as the mother and baby unit or the Rivendale unit, which worked with women with personality disorders... Our two principal criticisms of the prison were about the security and quality of the daily regime. Some aspects of security, such as excessive and cumbersome roll checks which impeded access to activity, seemed to be

*excessive and disproportionate to the identified risks…
That said, the activities on offer were too limited. We
found about a third of women locked up during the
working day and time out of cell generally was not good
enough. At weekends it was even worse. Our colleagues
in Ofsted judged the provision of learning and skills
provision as 'requires improvement', their second lowest
assessment… Nevertheless, this is a good report about
a capable prison. The issues we raise are eminently
fixable, and we hope the priorities we have highlighted
will assist ongoing improvement.*

Rose West was imprisoned for life in 1995 for her part in
the murder of ten girls with her husband Fred West. Fred
West was fifty-three when he hanged himself in prison
while awaiting trial in 1995. They had buried the bodies
of the girls at their home in Cromwell Street, Gloucester.
One of the girls they murdered was her eight-year-old
stepdaughter, Charmaine.

Rose has circulated widely through the British women's
prison system since the mid-1990s. She had been held
at HMP Bronzefield in Middlesex. Following a plot to
attack her with pool balls in a sock, she moved to Low
Newton in 2008. Unlike that move, prompted by the
threat of violence towards her, her move to New Hall was
described as a routine switch. 'Despite what she has done,
it is a traumatic experience when prisoners change jails
and the bosses want West's transition to go as smoothly
as possible.'

She was, of course, in Holloway too, and our brilliant contributor Vanessa looked after her for two or three months there. Vanessa frowned as she reminisced about her memories of Rose West.

'She was a difficult one. Her crimes were dreadful. She was found guilty of murdering ten women, one of whom was her stepdaughter. The media portrays her as this very violent, very evil psychopathic, very narcissistic, personality disordered person.'

Given her terrible crimes, we struggled to disagree with the media. Had Vanessa seen a different side to her up close and personal?

'When, in actual fact, I looked after her, she was segregated from the rest of the general population [at Holloway prior to her trial], and so she was down the segregation unit, which I was in charge of at the time. We looked after her for about six to eight weeks before she went off to trial at Winchester Crown Court.'

This was exactly what we were hoping for. Vanessa had spent weeks with Rose at Holloway and had obviously had plenty of time to laser her sharp brain on what Rose was really like.

Prison officers as a whole take these things with a pinch of salt. You have to in order to a) work with these people and b) we're probably one of the most cynical [types of] people going; we don't listen to 'mainstream media hype'. Also, to be a professional person, that's what you have to do. The way sometimes the media portrays murderers, rapists, whatever... Although the crimes are separate, and they are dreadful crimes, the actual person themselves: you'd think they'd have evil stamped on their forehead, which they actually don't. They don't have horns growing out of their heads. Sometimes I do think the media portrays those people as that.

We were all too familiar with that mythical version of Rose West from our extensive reading about her, although in fairness there is also an awful lot of non-sensationalised, measured and careful journalism and writing available about the Wests. It was apparent, though, that Vanessa had seen a serious disconnect between lurid tabloid headlines and the woman she met.

Rose West was very quiet, she was very, what I would call, a thinker. You could tell she was forever thinking something. She was very able to apply herself to pretty much everything we asked of her. If we got her out to clean, she'd clean. She never caused us any angst in looking after her. She came out on a nightly basis for an hour to watch the TV, because she was down there for her own protection, she wasn't down there for punishment. So, we used to get her out for an hour or so every evening to watch a bit of TV, because at that time there were no in-cell TVs. She was what I'd call an easy prisoner to work with.

Of course, we also wanted to know how Rose reacted when her husband, the serial killer Fred West, died. Incredibly, Vanessa was there working and looking after her on that crucial day. What happened?

I suppose it kind of really brought it home to me the day that Fred, her husband, died, which was New Year's Day. It was about 4 o'clock , getting dark. I happened to be working. I got a phone call from the communications room saying the duty governor was on the way down to see Rose West, and I said, 'Yeah fine.' And when he came down he came into the office where I was sitting and he said, 'I've got to tell Rose that her husband has committed suicide', and I said, 'Yeah okay, she's only in the cell opposite the office and I'll take you through to her', which was normal. The officer had the keys and the duty governor was quite used to people opening doors for them. I opened the cell door and Rose was sat on her bed reading and I said, 'Rose, the governor's got something he wants to tell you', and she was like, 'Oh right, yes.' He said, 'Rose, I'm really sorry to tell you that Fred, your husband, has committed suicide, and he was found just after lunch today in Winson Green prison.' And all Rose said was 'Oh, okay then.' That was it. No emotion, no nothing. This was allegedly the love of her life, there was actually nothing, no flicker of emotion whatsoever.

In point of fact, Fred West had been found hanged in his cell. We asked Vanessa whether the lack of normal reaction to her husband's suicide was because Rose didn't feel emotion or because she didn't want to show any? Vanessa saw it as a mixture of the two.

A bit of both. I also think that she thought, as did Fred, if he topped himself she'd get off, and I think she firmly believed that. They say psychopaths have no emotion, and clearly she had no emotion. There was an absolute blankness there. She certainly knew what was happening; you could see that she acknowledged it and took it in, but she didn't show any emotion, which I always thought was strange. I thought she'd have reacted more, particularly because of the fact that he had died and also the nature of how he died. But nothing.

After we had explored these fascinating inside details, Rose West also seemed as good a person to start with as any to answer one of the big questions our study of Wakefield and New Hall had led us to:

When do people become evil?

Vanessa's measured, but intriguing response will stay with us. 'When they do something that you can't comprehend or you can't understand. It's all very well saying someone was murdered by someone knifing them, but knifing someone, that takes an awful lot to be up close and personal with somebody and take their life from them.'

There are obvious exceptions to this, of course, like self-defence, but to go out with the intent to murder somebody for a heinous reason takes a lot and Vanessa has always questioned how someone could do that and become a serial killer. She acknowledged that some say it starts with killing animals in their youth; we had seen some of this in the history of Broadmoor patients. For her, sometimes this is the case, but sometimes not. In her experience, alarmingly, sometimes there are little to no signs. Vanessa has always been fascinated by what 'flips that switch', when someone becomes a serial killer.

'If I had the answer I'd possibly be worth a few bob.'

Everybody should be assessed on an individual basis. As we have seen, Geoffrey Wansell's vast experience led him to this same conclusion. Vanessa summarised what really struck her when looking after Rose West for two or three months at Holloway in the following terms:

'She was no bother. She is narcissistic and manipulative but she obeyed everyone, kept her head down, but she was very aware.' When the papers 'jazz them up to be personified as evil, to me that just makes them something bigger than they actually are'.

As Vanessa concluded, 'At the end of the day, when you're in jail you're in jail. It doesn't matter who you are or what you've done.'

It certainly seems likely that jail is where Rose West will stay. As Geoffrey Wansell put it to us: 'Rosemary West is exceptional, one of those cases, like Myra Hindley, where society could not bear for them to be released into society.

We say people can be rehabilitated but I accept that she is [the exception].'

What impact does the knowledge of this life term have on the psyche though? Geoffrey has done more than enough research to have an interesting take on this.

Rosemary West is like Levi Bellfield: they realise full well they are very unlikely to ever be released from prison and they make the best of it... but what do we as a society really have in mind? Is it an eye for an eye? The victim's families have every right to want revenge and retribution. We as a society have set our face against capital punishment, and I agree, but what then is the deterrent to the ultimate crime?

We wanted to know, from Vanessa's expert perspective on both female and male prisoners, whether there were any characteristics that she would associate with female and male psychopaths respectively. She had a ready response. When it comes to female prisoners in her view:

Many years ago female prisoners were considered 'mad not bad' as it was 'inconceivable' that women could cause such damaging crimes. Some people even today think that, and many female prisoners are taken to mental asylums instead of prison because 'How can a woman whose job it is to nurture and care for children end up murdering them?' If you did, you must be 'mad'. But you can't ignore that there are bad female prisoners.

Our research into New Hall's inhabitants certainly bears out her last sentence. Interestingly, part of the thinking she details here may well have come from Broadmoor. We know that in its earlier history, when it still admitted women, the vast majority of them had committed infanticide. These days they would be classified, in many cases, as suffering from lethally untreated post-natal depression. So, mad not bad indeed. Perhaps the lingering sense of injustice around this cohort has driven the thinking a bit too far in the other direction in the twenty-first century.

Returning to Vanessa, what other differences had she noted between women and men? 'Women have much more emotion in jail than men. Most of them are nurturers, they are carers, so they are worried about what's been going on outside, whereas a man will tend to worry more about himself inside the prison instead.'

She gave a gruesome and depressing account of the self-harm that is rife in the female prison community, which she has experienced first-hand and which has evidently had a profound effect on her. 'You get a lot more self-harm with female prisoners than male. A lot of that is because of abuse of female prisoners. In comparison, self-harm issues with women were much more severe than self-harm with male prisoners. Not to say that men aren't abused or don't self-harm, as they do, but it seems much more severe, in my experience, with women.'

Men may cut as a form of release, but with women Vanessa has seen women try to take their eyeballs out, bite chunks out of their wrists, shove biros into their legs and refuse treatment until it's almost turned gangrenous.

These are severe forms of self-harm.

Pete took a lot of gratification at New Hall from helping women who had come in abusing drugs and with sexually transmitted diseases, helping to get them cleaned up.

'It were awful to see, it was like seeing your daughter come into jail.'

Pete felt that he was resented for this as many of the staff saw prisoners as 'Pieces of shit that we shouldn't be helping. The attitudes were terrible at New Hall. I hated it. The prisoners used to call me "Pop" [Principal Officer Pete. POP]. New Hall was very different to Wakefield, but a lot more gratification.'

Like Vanessa, Pete had examples of truly horrific self-harm he was witness to. 'People who've cut their veins out' was most prevalent at his time at New Hall, and 'they'd bite lumps out of their arms, it were horrible to see.'

Jenny witnessed dreadful things as a prisoner, too. 'The self-harm was horrific. I've never seen so much. I'm talking so deep.'

She greatly respected those who would confidently walk around the prison with their arms out and their self-harm showing. 'Scars so deep they'd just missed the ligature.'

Some girls would scratch their own faces apart. Some officers, she would say 80 per cent, are very sympathetic and empathetic and would try to redirect prisoners to the listener service. The officers are not trained to deal with it all though.

'They're there to be prison guards, not to be mental health workers, otherwise they'd be in a different industry.'

There is mental health support available but there can be a waiting list. 'I think they could definitely do better, but they underestimate how much officers do take on as well.'

Doubtless in part to curtail the abuse that can lead to such serious self-harm, New Hall adopts a zero-tolerance policy towards physical and verbal threats, and can withdraw privileges if these threats take place.

* * *

Like Broadmoor's setting in the cutesy village of Crowthorne in Berkshire, or Rampton's incongruously close proximity to Sundown Adventureland, Nottinghamshire, HMP New Hall is set in picturesque Yorkshire countryside. Our contributor Vanessa visited New Hall numerous times. When New Hall first opened it was a satellite jail for Holloway. She would take prisoners that were convicted up to New Hall from Holloway, which was mainly a remand jail. Quite a lot of Holloway staff transferred to New Hall, too.

In addition to Vanessa's expert opinions, we were also keen to get John's view on contrasts between male and female prisoners. John opened his remarks by describing his involvement in New Hall women's prison. He explained that recently self-harm in female prisons was at such a high rate that the government was considering putting together a task force to deal with it. John stepped in and helped to manage self-harm at New Hall for three years, and it was the only female prison in the country where self-harm was reduced. He explained that most of the issue was due to management attitudes. 'You've got to make sure people have the right appetite for the job, otherwise they won't achieve'.

When asked to outline the main differences between male and female prisons and prisoners, John believed there were...

...lots of very, very subtle differences. Women, if I can generalise, women are very sociable things. If a man is going to escape, he'll plan his escape down to the last detail and work and work and work. Generally speaking, women don't do that. Generally speaking, they're a little bit more reactive. If a man's got a problem, he'll probably withdraw himself. Women tend not to do that. If a man's in prison and he's got access to drugs, he'll binge and go off his head and you'll know about it, because you'll probably have to get the ambulance in and there'll be all sorts of problems. Generally speaking, women might use substances as a coping mechanism.

On the dynamics of male and female friendships between inmates: 'Men will run with the pack, you'll get a group of men and they're all very similar and that's how they get on. You get a group of women, and they're all very, very different, but that's how they get on.'

John told an anecdote where he was asked to give

support on a wing where a prisoner had smashed up her cell and had been moved to the segregation unit as punishment. The officers on the wing had been happy to see her leave the wing due to the disruption she'd caused, but she was now begging to be let out of her segregated cell. In contradiction to his fellow officers' beliefs, John ordered the prisoner to be taken from segregation back to a regular cell. He explained to one of the officers:

> *Right, someone comes into prison, they're scared to death. They spend their first night in custody and it's the most uncomfortable thing that they've ever experienced in their life. They hate it, they've said they're in danger of self-harm and, to all intents and purposes, their behaviour is causing some concern. Let's say, take 'em out of prison and go home, the shock may very well be enough to prevent a recurrence of their offending. I'll tell you this, once they've been in prison for two or three days, they get used to it, and their confidence grows.*

Amongst other things, here John was describing to us the intriguing process of how an individual becomes institutionalised. Just as with a friendship or a workplace, once you settle in and start to relax, confidence and even complacency can grow and bad behaviour can potentially begin to creep in. It seemed to us as if at somewhere like Wakefield you want the prisoners to feel at home but not too at home. John's words seemed to chime in with this.

Whilst it's not ideal, they get a bit more comfortable, they start accepting the fact, then the opportunity to shock them and to maximise that and get something back is gone. So when that prisoner in that cell starts to settle, and starts counting the bricks on the wall and starts to settle down and gets used to the fact that they're in there, then being in the segregation unit holds no fear from them. So whilst they're screaming to get out, I'm going to get them out of that cell and go into their room and sit down with them and assess whether that fear for the segregation unit is real. And if it is real, I'll use that and put them back onto normal location, knowing that the threat of coming down to the segregation unit is more real than it was previously. Because they've had a taste of it.

Whilst the other officers believed that John was wrong, they could not argue with the results. The prisoner was fine from then on and did not have to return to segregation. John jokingly reflected that he would often tour prisoners around the segregation unit and scare them, showing them the rooms for highly difficult prisoners, which seemed to be effective. Looking back, he appreciated that the other officer didn't have enough experience to understand John's mindset, but as John stated: 'We don't get rid of problems, we manage them.' Had he kept the prisoner in segregation and allowed her to settle, it might have caused further problems in the future, but this method allowed John to manage her behaviour. He then explained that there are two reasons that people commit crimes: because they want to, and because they don't think they will be caught. He concluded:

'We teach people to understand the consequences of their actions. And that's not punishment, that's life.'

For Rose West, although in the end we could not be sure whether she had truly understood the consequences of her actions, and perhaps the sheer enormity and depravity of her crimes prevents that, by many accounts it seems as if she is keen to lead a quiet life of quiet pursuits, resigned to the fact that she will never be a free woman.

Chapter 14

Prison Transfers

As we've seen, Rose West has been transferred between various women's prisons. It got us thinking about the broader point of this potentially very dicey moment, possibly traumatic for prisoners and their guards alike.

Jo talked to us about the process of moving a prisoner: 'I took a con from New Hall to Rampton. They don't get released from Wakefield a lot. If they're moving to another prison, it's different to a hospital... if they were moving to Broadmoor, Rampton... From New Hall we moved prisoners to Rampton. I've been there once. Unless deemed otherwise they would go uncuffed, because they were under the Mental Health Act.'

Contributor Jim observed to us that many high-security institutions were interlinked due to their exchange of prisoners between prisons. He explained that there could be many reasons for a prisoner changing prisons, including a potentially dangerous falling-out with another prisoner, to access a specific course that another prison offers, or to get a different experience of the world during a sentence.

Vanessa described to us one prisoner that she transferred to New Hall. She called her the fake name 'Jane' for the purposes of the story.

She was in a wheelchair but she wasn't disabled. She said she was disabled but she wasn't. She used to accuse the staff of rape – female staff, male staff, didn't matter – she used to accuse them of rape. And of course, when she first started it there were big investigations, but then we realised that actually this is just 'Jane' being 'Jane'. And so she came to being transferred to New Hall jail and we got a taxi, a taxi was ordered. It wasn't me but it was two staff that I knew quite well that took her up to New Hall from Holloway. And halfway up the motorway, the taxi driver pulled over onto the hard shoulder and told the staff to get her out of his cab because she'd accused him of rape.

The jail got a phone call from the staff asking what to do. 'We can't be left on the hard shoulder with a prisoner in the middle of transfer.'

Vanessa had to tell them not to let the cab driver kick them out: 'She can't be dumped on a hard shoulder'. It was very strange but eventually they did get her to New Hall.

Vanessa recalls another transfer. That transfer involved six officers to one prisoner. This was unusual but the prisoner was very, very violent and had a history of assaulting numerous staff.

> *The traffic was horrendous. And the driver – we used to call them 'pixies' – they were like minibuses but they were like a Ford van and if you got sitting on the wheel arch, it was a very uncomfortable ride, you felt every lump and bump going along. We were fighting in the back with Gloria, and pixie driver decided that he was gonna blues and twos [lights and siren] it the entire way up the M1 to New Hall on the hard shoulder because the traffic was such, it was a Friday night, it was just at a standstill, and we literally blues and twos'd it up to Wakefield, to New Hall to get her up there.*

They took the prisoner (Gloria) to the segregation unit, which was, for Vanessa, 'the only time I saw the inside of the seg at New Hall. It was funny going to New Hall because it was like a mini Holloway – there's always banter between jails. It was interesting to see old faces. A lot of them were from Yorkshire, who transferred to get a ticket home.'

We surmised, correctly, that on the basis of what she had already said, Vanessa would be the perfect contributor to walk us through the whole basic process of a prison transfer.

'Most prisoners who are sentenced are transferred out of London jails to prisons for the convicted. The London jails – apart from Brixton – are all remand jails. After conviction, the prisoner goes back to jail and then over a week or even a month, he'll be looked at to see his offence, sentence, demeanour in prison, and it's then decided by those who deal with the transfers what prison he'll go to.'

So, she explained, somebody famous or first-time offenders, they are more than likely to go an open jail. If its violence or more serious offences, they won't go to an open jail. So, it depends on the offence.

'Nowadays it's done through private companies, but at the time it was conducted by prison staff. Much of the running around fell to whoever was youngest on the team: collecting the prisoner, making sure they were strip-searched, making sure they had all their property. Males would be handcuffed wrist to wrist with another prisoner.'

When Vanessa first started, females weren't handcuffed, then at some point they realised females could also escape! Consequently, it became standard practice that they too were handcuffed.

'When you arrived at the jail, you handed them over. The most important thing was to make sure you had the warrant with you. Other prisons can't accept a prisoner without a warrant. It's not a difficult process but it can be lengthy if a prisoner has a lot of property or doesn't want to move prisons, which can cause delays. However, most prisoners are happy to transfer and to get on with their sentence.'

Vanessa told us that they would usually transfer prisoners in batches of four or five at once with three staff. However, in the case of really violent or difficult prisoners, more staff would be assigned and the prisoner would be transferred solo.

One of the weirder Wakefield stories concerns Michael Sams' attempts to sue the prison for losing his artificial leg during a transfer. He was awarded £4,000 damages for the loss, much to the public's disgust when the story broke. He also brought a civil case against the prison, claiming that his bed was too hard, as well as claiming that artworks he had made in prison had gone missing and that being held in solitary confinement had unfairly led to loss of earnings.

Chapter 15

Prison Visits

To visit Wakefield, you must be on the visitor list of the person that you are visiting; you need to book your visit at least two days in advance, at least one visitor in the party has to be over eighteen years old, and of course, you have to bring the necessary ID with you.

All visitors, no matter what their age, are given a pat-down search, and if you are accompanied by children, you are not allowed to bring in pushchairs or car seats. There are lockers for valuables, and for each adult visitor there is a £25 maximum cash limit to use on food and drink in the visits hall. Anything you try to bring in is strictly controlled, plus one in ten visitors leaving Wakefield get selected at random for an exit search, which follows exactly the same procedure as the search everyone goes through on the way in.

Whether anyone is trying to sneak drugs into Wakefield is a point of particular interest. This means there is every chance you will be screened by drug detection dogs. If the dog finds anything dodgy, a few things can happen. You might have to conduct your visit under closed conditions. If you are found with drugs on you or if you get caught trying to traffic drugs inside, the visit can be cancelled. You might get a ban from visiting Wakefield for a certain period of time, or the police might even get involved if it is serious enough.

Forget that mini-dress, low-cut top or baseball cap, too. On the basis of what the prison calls its 'family-friendly dress code policy', you could get turned away for wearing anything inappropriate or any head covering other than those that religious practice necessitates.

Situated on a quiet street corner just outside the prison walls is the visitor centre at Wakefield, which has a play area in it and folding chairs pushed against the left-hand wall. A noticeboard creates a strange feeling of domesticity and familiarity, and it feels a bit like a doctor or dentist's waiting room.

At Wormwood Scrubs Vanessa oversaw and was responsible for visits at the prison. She pointed out to us that visits don't just involve searches and security but also accomodating the elderly and young children. 'You have got to be sensitive to all that whilst trying to stop contraband from coming into prison. There is a difficult balance between security and safety and decency. If someone really wants to get something in, they will. They create a diversion and will sneak things in whilst staff are distracted. You can't be in all places at once.'

In terms of the standard process, convicted prisoners

must send out a visiting order: you can't just turn up. If you're a category A those visitors are checked by the police and authorised. Prisoners usually get a visiting order once a month and a PVO – privileged visiting order – an extra visit. This makes the average one visit per fortnight.

By contrast, remands and un-convicted prisoners can have visitors that just 'rock up' without a visiting order. However, if it is a category A on remand, the visitor list needs to be approved. Most prison systems have a visitor centre run by PACT, a charity. PACT tend to sort out any issues for visitors, lockers and what they can bring in. They go from the visitor centre through the gate to visits.

Cat B and C jails might have a drug dog on duty that visitors have to walk past before entering. Cat A jails are more rigorous in terms of visitors being searched.

Convicted visits usually last an hour, whilst remand visits are usually half an hour as remand prisoners could have visitors every day. Most visitor areas have play areas for kids, and we have seen the one at Wakefield.

Policies differ between jails. Some have high tables, some have low, in some you have to have your hands on your knees at all times, and others you need to have them out on the table at all times, and some have barriers between prisoners and visitors; everywhere is different.

Likewise, at New Hall, visitors aged sixteen or older must prove their identity with an acceptable form of ID, before entering the prison. All visitors, including children, are required to have a pat-down search, and may also be sniffed by security dogs.

Any valuables must be left in a locker before entering the visitor area. An officer briefs you on the rules when your visit begins, and if you break those rules, your visit could be cancelled or you could even have a ban on further visits. The visitors centre, which New Hall describes as 'family-friendly', is open from 12.30pm to 2.30pm and offers information and support, as well as toys and activities for kids. The centre opens again at the end of the visit at 4pm, and it is also the place where future visits can be booked.

Pete started a major fundraising initiative which raised £360,000 through the National Lottery to build the New Hall children's play facility. He did the same at Wakefield and raised around £345,000 to help with the visits and the children's play facilities.

Vanessa has caught people sneaking in drugs through dirty nappies because no one thinks they'll be checked. You can bring in a baby bottle but the baby is checked. Visits can be a traumatic time and the job is to make that trauma seem as small as possible and to be sensitive to how visitors feel. Staff tend to be sensitive to the differing needs of families in Vanessa's experience, but it can be awkward.

'On one occasion both the wife and the girlfriend of a prisoner showed up for a visit at the same time. A very difficult dynamic to navigate and de-escalate! You have to accept that some people will find it incredibly difficult to visit somebody that they love in that sort of environment.'

Martin described other family visit issues, too. Sometimes if a family is too big and they all come and visit, you have to stagger their visits to around five at a time.

'When I was on visits for two and a half years, I never saw anybody argue, or particularly have a falling out apart from when it was people trying to bring drugs in and we were catching them. Most drugs are transferred through kissing orally.'

He noted the same practice as Vanessa had: 'Bringing drugs in in a child's nappy was quite an easy way of doing it. It was illegal for them to search a child under a certain age.'

* * *

Dr Maria Adams is an associate professor in criminology at the University of Surrey. We were keen to have Maria contribute to the book because of her research expertise around the experience of the families of prisoners, as well as food in prisons. She was awarded a PhD in 2017. Her thesis title was: *We are living their sentence with them... – how prisoners' families experience life inside and outside prison spaces in Scotland*. We were very grateful for her time and insights in writing this book. Maria was very well-placed to provide some interesting further context into aspects of parental relationships with prisoners, as well as the processes of prison visits.

Maria's research involved interviewing a range of family members, including parents, partners, uncles and grandparents. She also attended prison visits to observe interactions between family members. When discussing the social stigma associated with having a family member in prison, Maria noted that many family members chose not to disclose to friends and even other family members what was happening, meaning that often they were closed off from support and often didn't talk about it. As well as the emotional toll this would take on the family members, there was also the financial and social aspects to having a loved one incarcerated. Household responsibilities and childcare would fall solely on the family members on the outside, and often schools were not informed of their situation out of shame or embarrassment, so again support was often limited.

We asked Maria how parents might broach the subject of incarceration to their children. Often, if the child was young, they would be told that their parent was in the army or the hospital. If the child was slightly older, and more aware, they would understand the implications of being in prison, which would mean they felt the loss of their parent even more. In that way, many do experience a form of grief, which in some cases can have an impact on a child's mental health, resulting in conditions such as depression or anxiety.

When a person is in prison for a long time, Maria noted a deterioration in their relationship with their loved ones. It can be very difficult to keep in contact with someone whose means of contact is limited, especially if the prison is far away. Something of note is that this is often intensified for female prisoners. With fewer women's prisons in the UK, the probability of travelling further to visit family members is higher, putting strain on their familial relationships.

Maria pointed out further gender-specific needs for

women to us. Women are more likely to be single parents and to have caring responsibilities for children, whereas male prisoners are more likely to have someone else who is able to care for them while they're in prison, so often children of female prisoners are more likely to end up in the foster system. Furthermore, mental health issues and trauma from domestic violence rates are much higher in women's institutions.

She noted that prisons are often designed by men for men, and so the needs of women in prison are often not fully met. Maria's recent research has been looking into issues surrounding food in prisons; often the traumas experienced by female prisoners affects their eating habits, and eating disorders appear to be more specific to them than men. Many women use food as a way to control a seemingly uncontrollable situation, but more research is needed in this area. Due to these more gender-specific issues in female prisons, there is an emphasis on the importance of female friendships in prison; if there is a lack of emotional support from outside, prisoners are more likely to form emotional ties with fellow prisoners. But now let's get back to our main subject – prison visits.

What struck us is that there is, naturally, much about the process and procedure of it all, especially for category A prisons, that is similar to the process of getting inside Broadmoor. Maria's description aligns closely with our own experiences and with the descriptions given by other contributors.

As Maria explained it, any personal items, such as

phones and credit cards, must be left in a locker and are not allowed into the prison. Any money that is being brought in should be in coin form only. Often visitors are instructed to arrive half an hour to an hour before the allotted visiting time. Visitors are then called by name and are taken in in groups, which helps with the flow of the visiting hours.

When you enter the visiting room, there is one chair for the prisoner on one side of the table and several chairs for the visitors on the other side. The prisoners are not allowed to move from their seat during the visit. The only time visitors are allowed to move is if they head to the refreshments table. Depending on the category of the prisoner, there may also be a limit to displays of affection between the prisoner and their visitors; for example, some prisoners may not be allowed to hug or play with their children.

Prison officers supervise visitations and are watching every move to ensure that no one is attempting to give the prisoner any prohibited items. In that way, the environment is often quite intrusive; you are sat next to several other families and so it can feel extremely difficult to have those more private conversations. In some instances, fights can break out in the visiting rooms, which can be quite intimidating and can sometimes deter visitors. Overall, visiting rooms are not often family friendly. In many prisons (including, as we noted above, Wakefield) visitors are patted down regardless of age before entering, which can be quite off-putting.

Maria noted that often family members, particularly parents, are close to a young prisoner's case and are highly aware of the details of their offence. Whilst they might have their own personal feelings about their crimes, often these are put aside. Despite what they have done, they are still family.

For the eight and a half months that she was on remand, Jenny had almost daily visits at Bronzefield.

I'd have family, I'd have friends and all sorts… The officers would come and get you and take you to the visits area. You'd be patted down and then you'd wait in a holding room. Then you go and sit on a table and then the visitors come in from the other end. They are searched and then they'll come sit at the table, too. There's a cafe area where you can get food and drinks as a visitor. Times of visits vary. Some mornings you could have a two-hour visit and then during week they'd be an hour or hour and a half. Sometimes if the next visitor slot was empty, officers would let your visitor stay with you a bit longer. You get searched once the visit is done and then are taken back to your cell.

Even in this lighter security environment, Jenny described restrictions on intimacy, though. 'You can cuddle them [your visitor] but that's it. You were not allowed to cuddle for too long otherwise guards would tell you to get off, and you couldn't sit holding hands. It depends on officers. Some might let it slide and others would be really on it.

You could lean forward as long as not touching; it was quite intimate in that aspect.'

Chapter 16

Mind Games:
Radicalisation and
Manipulation

Of all the radicalised and manipulative coteries of prisoners to work their way through Wakefield, as Pete described them to us, the IRA were amongst the worst. Pete remembered IRA prisoners being on his wing at Wakefield.

'They were not allowed on the fours landing but would forever be trying to sneak up. At that time workers got paid in 50-pence pieces, so they were going around dealing tobacco, bookies putting bets on horses. They were very confrontational people because they thought that they were superior to staff and to the English.'

Pete recounted one attack to us, when an IRA category A prisoner kicked off in the servery during Sunday lunch. He kicked over a big urn of soup and gravy and then he started throwing food everywhere and assaulting the caterer. The officers had to intervene, 'sliding all over the flipping place'. Pete explained that, while now control and restraint is used, back then you just grabbed wherever you could. Pete was holding him by the legs and as they came up the stairwells, he kicked and Pete banged his head on the stairwell. Despite bleeding from a head injury, he had to take him down to the segregation unit, which was difficult as he was a big guy.

'He'd ruined the prisoners' lunch, and it were Sunday dinner. They loved Sunday dinner!'

One of the IRA sympathisers had contacted a solicitor and was trying to charge the officers who detained him with assault because of how he was handled. This threat hung over their heads for some time and the POA were involved. Nothing ever came of it but Pete says it was not a nice situation to be in. That prisoner was a 'nasty piece of work'.

Pete explained that a lot of staff had their families threatened by the IRA, too.

'They were very, very good at finding out who your family were and where they lived, how many children you had. They'd say: "You live at such-and-such street, your wife works at Morrisons, your two children go to such-and-such school." It were frightening times for the staff, and there weren't much support for them.'

Pete was told they would kill him but had to take it with a pinch of salt – he was threatened many times throughout his career, he was used to it: 'It's the nature of the job that we do'.

The demographic is changing, broadly from the IRA to

jihadists, but Wakefield has seen plenty of terrorists and political prisoners come through its doors. Jo noted to us that she witnessed a 'lot of radicalising in Wakefield: Levi Bellfield became a Muslim'. As we've previously heard, another Muslim convert was perhaps the most infamous prisoner of them all, the prisoner who currently goes by the name of Charlie Salvador but is still best-known as Charles Bronson.

Jo stated that a lot of the Muslims 'get together'.

'They form a clique and they like to recruit. They go for the weaker ones, but white people recruiting for gangs was stamped down. If your random search had more ethnic people in it, you had to answer for it.'

Martin had offered us interesting insights into religious conversions in prison.

Most prisoners with religious tendencies seek forgiveness and they don't get it from their religion so they try another religion and another religion… In the old days it was very rare or unheard of to change religion. Muslims, they don't really want people who are rapists and child molesters in their ranks. However, what they do is, if these people get into debt they take the debt off them and then they say, 'You've got to be a Muslim.' And then they say, 'You've got to go to Arabic classes and learn to be a Muslim.' Then they say, 'Right, if you want to be part of the family you've got to stab him or throw boiling water over him', and that's how they get it, and that's how these people can change religion.

We asked him about other religions, too.

'Quite a lot of people turn to paganism in prison. In Wakefield it was very difficult to get a pagan shaman [hofgothi] to come in. Quite often they were allowed to have meetings but they were on their own and led by themselves.'

One notable example of a political prisoner was Radislav Krstić, the Bosnian Serb war criminal. He was convicted of genocide for his role in the Srebrenica massacre when a general in the Serbian army. Krstić is over two decades into a thirty-five-year sentence imposed in 2001 by the international criminal tribunal for the former Yugoslavia (ICTY) in The Hague.

Just as his upbringing left Robert Maudsley with feelings of murderous intent towards those who had cruelly assaulted children, Krstić's role at Srebrenica attracted the attention of Islamic extremists within Wakefield. The Srebrenica massacre was the genocidal killing of over 8,000 Muslim men and boys, as well as the abuse and displacement of between 25,000 and 30,000 Bosnian women and children who were separated from their slain male relatives. This July 1995 atrocity in what is now Bosnia and Herzegovina had unexpected repercussions in a Wakefield prison cell many years later, in May 2010.

For one of our prisoners, this was a notorious incident, even in the annals of violent attacks at Wakefield:

The Serb general was nearly killed at HMP W. The Serb whose name I cannot pronounce was on D wing. He was in jail for war crimes. Mass killings of Muslims. Given the gang culture at HMP W and what he was in for, it was astonishing and poor management that the Home Office located him at HMP W. One of the attackers I knew very well. A Muslim by the name of Krasniqi. He was part of the Reading gang who abducted two young girls in the early 2000s as a revenge attack, gang related. They sexually assaulted and tortured the girls, killing one and shooting the other in the head. She was left in a Reading park and survived.

Krasniqi was on D wing. Another prisoner had just arrived from HMP Belmarsh the very day prior and he joined Krasniqi in the attack on the Serb. The two of them had the Serb in his cell for several minutes slashing him and stabbing him. Krasniqi walked out the cell and said, 'He is done [ie dead].' Indeed the Serb was nearly dead, he had lost so much blood. A now retired officer worked on him with medics and eventually got a pulse. He survived the attack.

I was with Krasniqi on many legal visits prior to his trial. I saw the police photos of the Serb's body and the injuries. They were horrendous. When Krasniqi went to trial he was forced to wear a bulletproof jacket as the prison service considered him to be at risk from the Serb general's friends in the UK. Krasniqi got life. In a huge failure by the HMP W, they relocated him and his co-defendant back onto the same wing together to then attack another inmate with a razor. Surely they should have been separated?'

Krstić's solicitor, Kate Maynard, described him as 'an unpopular and vulnerable prisoner', always a bad combination for inmates. For three Muslim fellow prisoners, Indrit Krasniqi, Ilyas Khalid and Quam Ogumbiyi, his notoriety for the massacre merited him having his throat cut. He barely survived this incident, and subsequently he suffered other attacks after he was transferred to HMP Long Lartin and HMP Woodhill. His Wakefield assailants were described in court as 'violent criminals with extremist views' and 'very dangerous', and they were in the same part of the prison as Krstić. At the Central London County Court trial, presided over by Antonio Bueno QC, all three were convicted of causing grievous bodily harm with intent. Krstić ended up with a very hefty compensation, with the Ministry of Justice picking up his costs and him being awarded £35,000 for trauma suffered and £17,500 for the physical wounds.

Wakefield came into the firing line, too. The judge called out the prison for lacking 'the appropriate facilities' to keep the notorious Serbian general safe from 'being brought into contact with very dangerous prisoners with obvious motives for harming him'. With two of the prisoners on the same wing as him, one of them had been moved into his unit only a day before the 7 May 2010 attack. At his trial in The Hague, Krstić had been initially sentenced to a prison term of forty-six years, reduced on appeal, and after an agreement that he spend some time in British prisons, he was transferred to a Polish jail.

In her summary response to his successful claim, his

solicitor Kate Maynard made a comment that stuck out for several reasons, when she stated:

> *Three fellow-prisoners… held him down and cut his throat. This was a retaliatory attack carried out by radicalised Muslim prisoners for Mr Krstić's role in aiding and abetting the massacre of Muslims during the civil war in Yugoslavia [charges he has continuously denied]. As the judge found, he was fortunate to escape with his life, albeit with permanent physical and psychological injuries.*

A number of our contributors have remarked on the process of conversion and at times radicalisation that they have witnessed inside Wakefield, including Jo Taylor. Were these three men, Islamists on arrival, radicalised even further inside the prison? In days gone by, the network of IRA terrorists in Wakefield and elsewhere begs the same question. Are these category A prisons hotbeds for radicalising the already radicalised? How can prison officers control this? A prisoner described to us how one white convert was the victim of a vicious attack.

> *Wayne Gasgoin was a traveller from the Hull area, serving a life sentence for multiple rapes of elderly old women. [There was a] Muslim attack. White convert Andrew Lloyd in a pre-planned attack hit him over the head several times on C wing in 2012. Wayne Gasgion lay there unconscious for half an hour before staff were*

alerted. I sat opposite leaning on some railings and watched it. Gasgoin spent weeks on life support and had open brain surgery. Not one witness would come forward and make a statement. I knew it was going to happen but said nothing. People do not inform or grass, a golden rule in prison. It was not my business.

Another Islamic terrorist and current Wakefield inmate is Kamel Bourgass, convicted of the knifing to death of police officer Stephen Oake; he also attempted to murder two other police officers. Bourgass is serving a life sentence. He was complicit in the Wood Green ricin plot, too.

We could not help noticing, too, in the story above, Krstić's continual denial of all the charges against him. Much like the famous line spoken by Morgan Freeman's character Red in prison movie *The Shawshank Redemption* – that he is 'the only guilty man in Shawshank' – Jo Taylor stated that 'everyone at Wakefield says they're innocent'. Krstić was obviously no exception.

* * *

Jo told us: 'It's more fun with the women, you can have banter with the women... It was alright with the women, they were just different; a lot of their crimes were theft, drugs. There were murderers... many of them actually domestic murderers retaliating after they'd been beaten, but you could have a laugh with them. It's not the same with men. You get people striking up friendships with prisoners, but you need to strike a balance.'

Jo told us that the refrain from prisoners about her style was:

'You were firm but fair Miss Taylor.'

She was also aware of some past incidents in which officers used force on prisoners.

'I didn't batter people. Some people did.'

Our orderly would come in and clean the office, make the tea, make a bit of toast in the morning. He was sad I was leaving. 'I said to him, "I never asked what you did." He was showing remorse at that. And he said he raped and murdered his girlfriend. I said, "Why did you do it" He said, "Oh, I was off me head on drugs."'

When we asked Vanessa if, in her experience as a governor and an officer, many prisoners had remorse for their actions, she chimed in with the chorus of denial.

'The most common response was, "I didn't do it, Gov. It weren't me!"'

She went on to reflect, 'Remorse I always thought was quite a private thing. Unless you were in that intimate one-to-one setting and you had that kind of relationship with them, they wouldn't necessarily be inclined to profess that. Unfortunately, you don't get that kind of rapport with a prisoner in that way. They would most likely talk about anything like regret/remorse in some kind of group forum or therapy-type setting.'

She mentioned Jackie Molton, who runs an AA style group where they talk through things like that about remorse and their offences etc. She believes that is the area to have those feelings and those kinds of conversations.

Vanessa has had some prisoners say they 'shouldn't have done that' or maybe that wasn't the best idea and so on, but as she says: 'Is that remorse or is that just because they got caught? I don't know.'

We wanted to know if Martin had encountered some prisoners who did appear to genuinely regret their crimes.

'A lot of them – drug dealers, robbers, people like that – it's an occupational hazard they might go to jail, so they accept that. Sex offenders it's more difficult.'

He remembered one prisoner who had a shocking childhood of abuse. 'His father had been raped by his father, and his father and his uncle raped him, and he raped his child. Now for him that was normal behaviour. So, how do you then teach somebody that that behaviour that was normal to them isn't normal to everybody else?'

That's where psychologists come in and try to help change how prisoners like him see things.

Martin said that he did meet some prisoners who were remorseful and genuinely sorry, but for 'most of them it was normal behaviour'. He offered the example of a young child playing in her pants at the beach. A normal person would see that and think it was just a child playing, how sweet. A sex offender, though, might see that as the child egging them on, encouraging them to make a move.

'You've then got to break that behaviour.'

One Wakefield inmate known for protesting his innocence more than most is Jeremy Bamber.

Bamber is currently in Wakefield serving a life imprisonment with a whole life tariff after he was found guilty of killing his adoptive parents and sister and his sister's two little children. He's spent nearly forty years behind bars but still campaigns for his release, protesting his innocence. He has even won over some individuals who have done their research into him. For example, Eric Allison, a reformed criminal himself who became the *Guardian* newspaper prison correspondent, was in contact with Bamber for many years and died in 2022 convinced of his innocence.

Jeremy Bamber's birth name is Jeremy Marsham. He was born on 13 January 1961. In 1985, the so-called 'White House Farm' murders took place in Tolleshunt D'Arcy, Essex. The dead, as a result of the sick killing spree, included Bamber's parents, Nevill and June Bamber, sister Sheila Caffell and her six-year-old twin boys, Nicholas and Daniel Caffell. When the case got to court, a majority (not unanimous) guilty verdict was reached. After committing the murders in order to secure a large inheritance, Bamber placed the rifle in twenty-eight-year-old Sheila's hands. A diagnosed schizophrenic, he tried to pin the awful crimes on her by making it look like a murder-suicide.

Bamber has obsessively maintained his innocence. What remains of his family consider him to be guilty. His case was referred to the Court of Appeal in 2001 by the Criminal Cases Review Commission (CCRC), but his conviction was upheld in 2002. The CCRC then rejected further applications from Bamber in 2004 and 2012. In 2012 the Commission stated that it had not identified any new evidence or legal argument that could raise any real hope of his conviction being overturned. Then in March 2021, a new application came once again to the CCRC, for a referral to the Court of Appeal, which was also rejected. With thirty-eight years behind bars this year, he is one of the longest-serving prisoners not just in Wakefield but in Britain.

Not a popular inmate, even by the generally low standards of popularity enjoyed by the prisoners of Wakefield, one prisoner had a great deal of hugely entertaining detail about Bamber and his life inside that they were willing to share exclusively with us.

Jeremy Bamber – what a character he is. He is very manipulative and controlling. Many offenders believe he is guilty. He is on C wing at HMP W. He actually believes he is above other prisoners. He has his supporters who are fooled by him, they send him stamps and money in. He is called arrogant, he is rude and even with his so-called innocent stance he will never get out.

We had heard from other sources too about this strange group of outside supporters that has clustered around Bamber and communicates with him inside. He is also reputed to have got close to several female fans during his lengthy incarceration.

This rather inexplicable fandom does not seem to extend inside the prison, where he has been seriously attacked at least twice. On one occasion he had to have twenty-eight stitches in his neck after he was attacked while he was making a phone call. Another time, he was forced to defend himself with a broken bottle when another prisoner shanked him. We wanted to know from a prisoner themselves why he was so hated.

The public see the documentaries on him and some actually fall for this, but when you have met him, lived with him over a long period, the true Jeremy surfaces. The act can be played out on the phone calls, in his letters [which are well written, he is very articulate], and even on a visit he can come across as poor me. However when you live with him it is so clear to see. He now has grey hair, still has good hair, he wears glasses these days, slightly overweight. His cell is like a tip, full of junk and papers. He is very rude to staff. By example, when his cell is searched he will insist all his legal papers are sealed in a bag in front of him to ensure staff do not read them. This infuriates staff as it is not needed.

Back to his character, he has been seen to mock the very people who write to him and send him money, so this says a lot about his character. In short, a very horrible man and this is the opinion by many inmates. He has no backbone to challenge people if he is abused, he will just walk off. A lot of inmates torment him about the silencer found at the scene. He took off the silencer and hid it after the murders. There was no way his sister could have shot herself with the silencer on the gun. A lot of people will shout out to him about this, 'You fucked up on the silencer.' He hates it. He has been assaulted over drug debts, but nothing serious and in general he is left alone and not considered a target by other inmates. Not many will engage with him.

It seems that many prisoners are wise to the manipulation of their fellow inmates. We also wanted to know, however, how staff could detect the signs and tactics that they were being manipulated. Vanessa told us that being manipulated can happen to anybody in jail, be they staff or prisoners.

'It usually starts with chatting. You have to talk to prisoners as part of your job to build up a rapport and professional relationship with them. A lot of people can't understand it. Many believe we should lock them up and throw away the key, but it will never work like that. At some stage you have to unlock that person and let them out into society.'

The catalyst for the manipulation could be something as simple as when she used to smoke in the exercise yard. An individual prisoner would start talking to her and ask if they could have a fag. She soon learned how to frame a response to this.

I would say, 'If I give you one, I've got to give 343 cigarettes, because I don't pull you out as anything special.' You've got to cut them dead. Some people might give in, and that's how it starts. 'Oh Gov, I've missed the last post, can you take this out on your way home and post it?' Once you get into a routine where everybody wants a little bit of you to get something, it's a very slippery slope. Myra Hindley manipulated a governor to take her to Regent's Park and get an ice cream. That's how manipulative Myra Hindley was.

She went on to make a point which chimes closely with our understanding from the prisoners, too, about how manipulation can grow.

'Prisoners have one thing more than we have, and that's time. They have time to sit and watch people and see which ones are vulnerable, those of us they think are vulnerable, those of us they think can be exploited, those of us who may stick out.'

Vanessa gave the example that she recalled of a woman on trial who wore her own trousers to work rather than uniform. This was not specifically speaking forbidden, she was allowed to do so, but it marked her out as against the grain. Prisoners can smell this and will single people like that out as different, potentially someone to manipulate.

'Many, many prisoners are predatory outside, what's stopping them from being predatory inside? Nothing. That's why you have to have good training, good support, and you have to have a mechanism where staff can report instances, any instances, and aren't seen to be "Oh well, get on with it!" It has to be taken seriously.'

Of course, one form of manipulation is ingratiating yourself with prison officers, and surely one way to do this would be by acting as informants for prison workers. Do 'snitches' exist, we asked Vanessa next. She didn't let us down with her story.

She told us how she went on a London course and worked with the police to bring 'CHIS' into prisons. A CHIS is a Covert Human Intelligence Source. In other words, a snitch. She confirmed that prisons do run them but it is very difficult to orchestrate. With the police outside, you can meet anywhere to relay information, but within the walls of a prison there's very few places to meet with the CHIS to relay the information they have without getting caught or raising any eyebrows.

'Above all else you have to ensure the safety of that CHIS. If anybody found out about it, there would be hell to pay.'

She explained that some people do it for reward, whether that's an extra packet of fags, or good reports to judges, but it needs to be very securely controlled and managed. It can be extremely rewarding but also extremely dangerous.

Our contributor Martin was also very familiar with prisoner manipulation techniques, and talked to us about conditioning. 'With young prisoners you'd have to constantly watch your back, but with older prisoners they'd try to condition you over a longer period of time and get you to think a behaviour was normal when it wasn't.'

There was a different way of dealing with prisoners which Martin had to get used to. It was difficult, he told us:

You have to know when you're being played, and somebody that's really clever and has done twenty-odd years in prison has a pretty good angle on most people's natures. So what I did, my modus operandi was, I'd be different every day. I'd say 'Hello' to somebody one day and then the next day ignore them. Then they'd come to me and say, 'What's wrong?' 'Oh nothing, why did you think there was something wrong?' So I made myself unpredictable, and they don't like unpredictable people. I didn't have a problem, but they found it far harder to condition me.

Their primary tactics in conditioning were 'mainly wanting things'. Many of the times the officers would say no to the prisoner, so the prisoners wouldn't go and speak to the officers to ask, they would jump the chain of command up to PO or governor. But they should go to their officer, if they say no go to the next level up and so on.

When I went there that never happened, but gradually that was enforced. If a prisoner came up to us [the orderly officer group] on the wing and said, 'Oh can I do so and so?' I'd say, 'Well what does your line manager say, what does your officer say?' 'Well, he said I couldn't do it.' 'Well,' I'd say, 'what did the SO say?' 'Well I haven't been to see him.' 'Why not? Don't speak to me, go and see your SO.'

By these methods, Martin tried to reinforce the correct line of management and to prevent prisoners from going straight to the governors with a problem. Some prisoners were trying to work the system to get things they weren't necessarily entitled to. He was keen to empower everybody:

giving the officers the power to say yes or no and reinforce the system, to keep everybody happy.

Chapter 17

Prison Breaks, Riots and Attacks

Despite the sophistication and commitment displayed in these tactics, sometimes prisoner behaviour at Wakefield and elsewhere as described to us has still gone very, very badly wrong.

That said, as far as we know, only one man has ever escaped Wakefield prison: Séamus Murphy. An IRA hitman, he successfully broke out many decades ago, on 12 February 1959. He owed his escape to a group of Irish republicans, who staged a daring rescue attempt. The group was formed by elements of both Saor Uladh, an Irish republican paramilitary organisation and splinter group of the IRA, and some members of Eoka, the Cypriot revolutionary nationalist entity. Later, Murphy recounted his escape in a book of his experiences. *Séamus Murphy, Having it Away: An Epic Story of Freedom, Friendship and IRA Jailbreak*. He went on to live to eighty outside captivity.

At the time of the jailbreak, he was a few years into serving a life sentence for his part in an IRA arms depot raid, which had taken place in 1955 at Arborfield in Berkshire. The raid was a big success from the gang's perspective, with plenty of weapons obtained that could be used against the British Army in Northern Ireland. The ringleaders had managed to escape, but the decision by Séamus Murphy, Joe Doyle and Donal Murphy to stay behind to sort some remaining issues led to their capture. They were all arrested, charged and handed life terms.

In his book he explained that he was not the only prisoner who was intended to be broken out. 'There were five men that had been earmarked for the escape. Two of them were Eoka men, another two were IRA, myself and Joe Doyle, while there was also a fifth with us, Tony Martin, who had deserted the British army in Cyprus and fought on the side of Eoka before he was arrested.'

However, it was only Murphy who ended up escaping. As we have seen, there are multiple measures put in place to ensure that this never happens now. We asked our contributor Jo what the consequences of such an escape would be for the institution if it were to happen today?

'That recent prison break at another prison [Wandsworth]? Wakefield would have lost their category A status and the governor would have been sacked.'

When we first met Jo, the audacious, very filmic HMP Wandsworth prison break was very much still in the news. On the morning of 6 September 2023, Daniel Abed

Khalife, only twenty-one years old and a former soldier, allegedly escaped from the category B prison.

He was working in the prison kitchen, wearing a cook's uniform, when the allegation goes that he used bedsheets to tie himself under a food-delivery truck in order to make a getaway. Khalife was on remand while waiting to go to trial on charges of terrorism. His escape sparked both a media frenzy and a hardcore national police search. A few days later, he was captured in the Northolt area of London, while riding a bike, by a Metropolitan police officer.

Concluding her reminiscence, Vanessa took a broadly positive stance. 'I would do it all again. I met some incredible people, both workers and prisoners. There are some, through one thing or another, who have ended up in jail.'

She does not believe that these individuals are the 'monsters' they are often wrongfully thought to be.

John has had the good fortune in his decades of service not to be involved in a prison break, but that is by no means the only sort of major incident that can happen in a high-security prison. In this context, he reflected that there are several things that officers aren't really prepared for when beginning a career in prison work, which he wishes to develop awareness for. The three main aspects are: managing death in custody, whether that's through natural causes or suicide; dealing with prisoners who are victim to assault; and how to manage prison disturbances. We consider suicides, and their prevention in custody, in Chapter 12, but we were keen to probe him on prison disturbances and prisoner assault.

He noted that when there is potential for confrontation, 'you get three chances before it gets rough'.

Skills need to be quickly developed to manage them. In situations where things go awry, John believes that there needs to be more conversations where officers are invited to reflect on what they could do better should they encounter the same situation again.

This discussion of reflection led John to recount the first prison incident he was personally involved in. He described Wakefield as 'quite an eerie place'.

'You can smell the atmosphere. It's in the air. You can cut it with a knife on some occasions, and then there are times when you can go into work and you won't stop laughing from walking in to walking out and you can have a great shift.'

Unfortunately, this would be one of those shifts. As John observed, seemingly small interactions and matters can become magnified under prison conditions.

'Prisoners will fight each other over a Mars Bar in prison. Mars Bars used to be tantamount to currency at one time!'

He explained that people in prison are keen to protect their survival. If there is an opportunity to boost their self-esteem, or reputation in the prison community, they will do it… there's a high likelihood that officers will often be the victim of that.

Beginning to tell this foreboding story, John recalled that he had only been at Wakefield for around three months: he would have been twenty-four years old.

As he put it, he 'stuck out like a sore thumb' amongst the other officers. The officers were in the process of locking up the prisoners for the night. They would proceed down the landing one door at a time. This was a strict schedule, so prisoners knew when to return to their rooms, where they would meet the officer, when they would say goodnight and when they would then lock in. On this occasion, the prisoner in question might have been new to Wakefield and so was not used to such a regimented routine.

When John reached his room, the prisoner was not there, so John shouted for him. When the prisoner still didn't come, he shouted for him again. When he appeared, twenty-two years old and just over five feet tall, he was not happy that John had shouted for him, and continued to verbally abuse and berate John. John recalled to us that he called him 'YTS'. Those of us of a certain age will recall that YTS stands for Youth Training Scheme, so this prisoner was referring to John being like an inexperienced school pupil and 'wet behind the ears', as well as offering more intense verbal insults. This was the first time John had been spoken to in such a way, and he was extremely shaken. In his pre-navy days, he reckoned he would have punched the young prisoner, but he refrained and did nothing.

Later, he confided in a fellow officer about what had happened, and the officer gave him some career-altering advice. The officer informed John that other prisoners had witnessed the confrontation, and if they saw another prisoner trying to condition an officer into accepting abuse, they would try to do the same. In order to regain authority and control, John would have to speak to the prisoner. He was instructed not to be aggressive, but to be clear that the prisoner's behaviour would not be tolerated.

Despite being nervous, John, accompanied by two other officers, went to the prisoner's cell. John gathered himself and said: 'Look, we've got to get on in here, this is about respect. I will absolutely not tolerate that again. I've cut you a bit of slack but it's not on.'

John was able to set things right. After that conversation, there were no further issues with that prisoner. Crucially, John noted that had he not had that core and supportive conversation with the other officers, he may not have come back the next day. Either that, or he would have shied away from future difficult situations, which would have drastically altered the trajectory of his career. Looking back on the situation, John says the encounter was not a big deal compared to later experiences.

He proudly stated: 'I've never walked away from anything. And I wasn't prepared to walk away from that young lad. There had to be a way to deal with it.'

This elegant de-escalation is revealing of John's good personal qualities and approach, which also radiated in all our interactions with him. However, it is not always possible to diffuse things with a pragmatic, firm but fair approach. As this conversation from just three months into the job would imply, John faced a series of very difficult situations throughout his career.

As he revealed, some of these difficult situations

concerned some of the most high-profile prisoners that he interacted with at Wakefield. He shared one anecdote about a prisoner known as 'Paddy Kelly' (Paddy was not his first name, but this is how he was referred to), an Irishman who showed a distaste for the serial killer Dennis Nilsen.

Supposedly, every time Paddy saw Dennis Nilsen walk past the wing, Paddy would exclaim, 'Oh I don't like him', though almost comically. This disdain wasn't because of Nilsen's grotesque, murderous history, but rather his fame! 'I can't believe he gets all the publicity and all the notoriety, and I've killed far more people than he's killed, it's unfair!'

Paddy would then explain that when he was a 'vagrant' in London, he used to push tramps in front of trains, boasting that he had killed loads. When reflecting on this, John remarked with a sense of dark humour, 'communities thrive on a bit of competition'.

We know from our inmate contributors, however, that things can get wildly out of control despite staff's best efforts at de-escalation. One prisoner gave us an unforgettable description of just how fast things can kick off in the febrile environment of the exercise yard, even amongst 'friends'.

The exercise yard is a very volatile area and I've seen wars break out over the most petty incidents. On one occasion I saw a black male from the black gang push another black male who was in a wheelchair [a gang member previously shot on the outside]. The man pushing the wheelchair by pure accident pushed the wheel of the chair over a Muslim's foot. This [was] because all the Muslims were standing in the way. The Muslim took offence and hit the man who was pushing the wheelchair, all the blacks saw this and joined in to support their friend. There was twenty fighting and only two staff standing on the other side of the gate. The alarm bell was raised but no staff entered the yard until they had suitable numbers and dogs.

After this there were other attacks as a result of this. Blacks on every wing [would] fight Muslims. Even people who were friends, the Muslim and the black guy was friends prior, but because of the gang affiliation they even turned on each other. It was crazy. The to-and-fro attacks went on for three weeks until leaders from each side met on the yard to sort it out and stop it. A peace deal was done and it ended, but that is one example of how dangerous HMP W actually is.

Staying on the subject of violence, I have personally witnessed and been involved in. I am in prison for heinous crimes, I can be considered a target. I joined a Muslim gang against my family's wishes. I was attacked by a Muslim, lucky for me I sustained no injuries, a fat lip, I played the system and received over £6,000 compensation because I claimed I was stabbed in the mouth and had no feeling in my cheek. There was a price for my membership.

It wasn't just the exercise yard where things could kick off. Pete described to us that, with twelve officers, an SO and a PO, there would be three positioned on each landing. Prisoners used to have to slop out buckets as there wasn't internal sanitation and often got covered in faeces and urine. This in turn could cause fights to break out.

Another instance, which Jim discussed as an example of long-term, strategic management of prisoners, is the handling of a disturbance. He noted that the response to any form of disturbance must simultaneously deter future disturbances from occurring, but also mitigate against any grievances with prisoners. Only in that way is it possible to navigate a path towards effective interactions on an ongoing basis, and deal with them for the foreseeable future. He describes this kind of forward thinking as essential to the job.

When asked about what professionalism means to him, John responded with an inspirational and hard-hitting statement.

I suppose nobody wants to go to war. Nobody wants to be in a situation where you have to kill another human being... It's all great fun when you're going through basic training and they're showing you how to use a gun, but when you've missed them the first two or three times and they're still coming towards you and you have to get the knife out of your pocket, and you've got to kill somebody with your bare hands, it's all right in a pub setting saying, 'Oh yeah I wouldn't think twice about doing that.' And it's marvellous being a doctor and being able to cure people and help people, but when you've got to sit down and have that conversation and tell someone that they've got a week to live or a fortnight to live, or give people the worst news in the world... Being a professional is about having to do those things, that may seem to be distasteful. It's the least popular aspect of the job, but it's about doing it, and it's about doing it decently and doing the right thing.

John then went on to discuss how to manage conflicts within prisons. He outlined that there are three areas not to mess with to prevent confrontations: 'People's food, people's visits, and their communications.'

He then emphasised that it's especially important to avoid any form of confrontation within communal dining areas, as it may impact other prisoners' ability to receive food, which could cause further issues. 'When men are hungry they're like a pack of wolves.'

Most of us will be familiar with the almost cliched TV and movie depiction of a prison riot kicking off either in a jail dining area or a prison exercise yard, and it appears to be totally borne out by reality.

John shared an anecdote where he had to deal with a potential conflict. It did not occur at Wakefield, but the type of confrontation management that was deployed, he found completely transferable.

A prisoner had been complaining about the quality of the food for everyone to hear, shouting, 'The food is shit, I wouldn't feed that to my bloody dog.' John, as the principal officer on shift, told him he would sort it out and invited him to his office. This was a tactic to get him away from the dangerous dining area so as to avoid a public confrontation. Once he was inside, John asked the prisoner what was wrong. After further complaining about the food, John asked the prisoner to pass him the plate, which he did. John asked for his cutlery which he also passed over.

We had a conversation about where he was from and who he was and how long he'd been at the prison and so forth. Anyway, the door opened and an officer said, 'Come on lad, it's lockup time.' And he says to me, 'Hang on, what about my dinner?' and I say, 'What about your dinner? I've eaten it.' He says, 'You can't do that!' and I say, 'You just told me it was shit and you wouldn't feed it to the dogs! You've given it to me, you've passed me your knife and fork, I've bloody ate it, it was super!' And he says, 'Well, what am I gonna eat?' and I say, 'Well you were complaining that it was shit and you wouldn't feed it to the dogs, what you need to do kid, is go to lockup and think twice before giving your dinner away next time!' And he looked at me and he smiled and then off he trotted. And it was fine, it was absolutely fine.

In order to avoid other conflicts surrounding food, John would often have lunch in the dining hall and would queue up with prisoners and eat lunch with them. On one occasion, he recounted to us how he tactfully ate with prisoners in order to prevent a potential incident.

John: 'What are you doing with the carrots?'

Server: 'There's some black bits on some of the carrots.'

John: 'I only want carrots with black bits on.'

Server: 'Really?

John: 'Yeah.'

Server: 'Oh… alright' [passes him more carrots with black bits on].

Server: 'Why do you only want the carrots with black bits on?'

John: 'Because when this group comes through, that's all they're gonna complain about. And you tell them, the governor's had a plateful. And it's fine!'

'And I had a superb lunch with black bits on my carrots. To stop a riot.'

In addition to showcasing some world-class prisoner- and people-management skills, this amusing anecdote also recalls our experience of Broadmoor patients, in which mass killers would complain about tepid hot beverages or the quality of the Christmas dinner choice as if they were at The Ivy rather than a high-secure psychiatric hospital for the criminally insane.

There can be deeper psychological reasons for prison riots and unrest as well, though. Hayley's work with the Braille Unit at Wakefield convinced her that, if you remove hope and purpose from prisoners' lives, these things will happen: 'Prison riots happen when a sense of injustice is felt and people are bored and have nothing to do.'

We wanted to know of Lisa, when the worst does happen what protocols are in place for a major incident? At the time Lisa was there, certain officers would have radios that included all managers. During an incident those with radios would press a button to sound the alarm. The control room would then send staff out to deal with the incident. There were alarm bells situated everywhere. Staff members also had the 'old fashioned' whistle they could blow in the event of an incident.

Quite often if two prisoners were fighting, prisoners would walk away and wouldn't want to get involved. The ones who did see the incident would often say they never saw anything. They didn't want any involvement at all. This is borne out by our prisoner account a few pages back.

It was also very rare for a prisoner to assault a member of staff, and in Lisa's eyes, 'That was one good thing about Wakefield.'

For Lisa, it was something that made Wakefield stand out from other prisons where staff assaults were more prevalent. There was a riot only a couple of months after Lisa had joined Wakefield. That was during the time of the Strangeways riots. There were concerns that a riot would break out at Wakefield. 'A lot of prisons had rumours going round that the prisoners at that prison were going to cause trouble.'

People were scared the same thing would happen again at other prisons.

Lisa told us that 'Security had information that it was going to happen at Wakefield.'

This was around a week after Strangeways started. There was a staff protocol in place just in case. Word got round to the prisoners as well.

About five minutes before lockup the atmosphere changed on the wing. It was quite bizarre, a very quiet atmosphere. That's the noisy time, you know, because people are moving about. And it was very quiet. And then, there were myself and two other colleagues on the landing, we just tried to act as normal. And then a lot, I would say around thirty prisoners surrounded us. Now at first we were like 'This is not good.' But then talking to the prisoners, they were there to protect us. Which was quite bizarre. If a riot did happen, they were going to protect us, they weren't there to harm us, they were there to protect us. Now that was very, very unique. Very bizarre, but again that was the good rapport between staff and prisoners.

The riot attempts never happened. 'It was very powerful.' Her colleague, who had been in the service over thirty years, remarked that he'd never seen anything like that in his career before.

On a different note, her husband Paul told us how he witnessed a vicious scissor attack on a prisoner in Wakefield.

I think we were on an evening duty on C wing. We had an office where there was a barred cabinet with tools in it, and in the cabinet was a pair of scissors. The person in question came and asked for the scissors, so what you did was you gave them the scissors and signed them out, gave him the scissors and off he trotted. But what we didn't know was what he was going to do, which was walk up onto the next landing and stab another prisoner in the top of the head with them. Which is what he did. So obviously all hell broke loose.

The perpetrator was restrained and taken to the segregation unit, where he never came out; he was taken to a close supervision centre, where individuals don't mix with anybody else. The victim was taken to hospital and survived despite the injury to his head. 'He was quite lucky to be fair.'

On another shocking occasion, the prisoner in question asked a female officer to unlock his door, and when she did he basically pushed her inside, took her hostage, and held her there all night until the following morning.

'They ended up having to intervene because it became apparent that he was going to inflict some harm on her. So they sent a team of officers in to rescue her. The prisoner was restrained. Physically she was okay but was mentally never the same again.'

Lisa had given us the further disturbing context to this that he was a prolific rapist, which was part of the concern.

Paul recalled a time he too was also assaulted by a prisoner.

'When I was working down the segregation unit. A prisoner came down for his lunch and basically attacked me with a sock full of batteries, he hit me round the back of the head. I don't even know to this day how I managed to avoid it, I think it was just instinct that I was able to duck out of the way, so he didn't catch me properly, it was more of a glancing blow because I moved out the way just as he went to hit me. That weren't much fun.'

As it happens, Paul got on really well with this prisoner so it came as a shock. He apologised afterwards and said the only reason he had done it was because Paul was in charge, the SO at the time.

'It would have been anybody, anybody who was stood there at the time were gonna get it, and it just happened to be me.'

Paul accepted his apology. 'He wasn't gonna go anywhere, you had to find a way of dealing with these things. Basically, talking to him about it was the way to get round why he did it because obviously we did have quite a good relationship. He explained it to me and, well, I can't say I understood his rationale because I didn't. He wasn't a very well man to be fair.'

Paul and the prisoner were then fine after that. 'He used to find it quite embarrassing because we used to joke about it, and have a laugh together.'

Although it's not a Monster Mansion story, we could not resist including John's extraordinary account of his involvement in the Manchester Strangeways riots, which started in the chapel at Strangeways on the morning of April Fool's day 1990.

We got a shout at Wakefield saying Manchester had gone, and they had to send some, bucket-loads, of staff to go down and help 'em out. Half past eleven we got that telephone call, just going off-duty and nobody believed them! They thought it was an April fool! Half the staff went home! They went 'Oh no, we aren't having that.' Anyway, they were walking out the jail and there was a single-decker bus, a big coach, outside. And the staff were walking past the coach and they said to the coach driver, 'What are you here for?' He says, 'It's kicked off at Manchester.' 'Really?!' So we all got on the bus. We all thought it was an absolute joke! When we got to Manchester, it was horrendous, it was absolutely not a joke.

They were tasked with getting out all the prisoners who wanted to come out and doing it straight away. There were lots of staff utilised in bussing prisoners from Strangeways to other prisons around the country. They were getting in food from Manchester Airport to feed everybody, too, using contingency plans that they'd hoped they'd never have to.

We took the first bus, we took some prisoners to Birmingham, I remember being on the bus. We used to have a prison officer at Wakefield [Colin], absolute giant of a man, his hands were twice as big, he was absolutely huge this chap. And he used to do a lot of charity work and get involved in concerts. And at Wakefield at the time, they used to have a charity called Poachers [Prison Officers Association Charity], and every year they would do a party. The staff at the prison used to work alternate weekends, they used to work red division or black division, and they did two concerts. They did one for red div, and one for black div. And this bloke, he always used to do a bit of a comedy routine. I'm sat with the officer on the back of the bus, next to the emergency exit. We've got a wooden truncheon up our sleeves, because we wanted to be able to draw it really quickly if there was any issue; there's a senior officer at the front of the bus and two policemen, and we've got about fifty prisoners out of Strangeways on the bus. Don't know who we've got, we just got fifty prisoners.

We've pulled out of the main car park and this policeman at the front says, 'Stop the bus!' They'd got on the bus when their inspector were there. We'd gone round the corner, they said we gotta stop. The bus stopped, they said, 'If you think we're travelling a hundred odd miles to Birmingham on a bus with fifty prisoners with no handcuffs, you got another thing coming' – and they got off the bus! There's two of us on the back of the bus, one at front sat next to the driver, and fifty prisoners, no handcuffs. Nothing. It was not good. And the prisoners, they've turned round and they're leaning on the seats and going 'Bloody carnage in there, boss! They're murdering them, they're killing all the sex offenders!' And I said, 'Colin [his fellow officer], I think we might have got some perpetrators on here, some murderers.' And he said, 'I know, everything will be alright.' I was only a young officer.

He'd got the radio on, flying down the motorway, every time a decent song comes on the radio, the bus was swaying, they were in the aisle dancing. They thought it were a day out! Like they were going to Blackpool on a club trip. Anyway, we had to pull in for fuel, whether we wanted fuel or not, because there was just a convoy of buses. There must have been fifty police cars and fifty bobbies all lining the route; we all went in in a line, whether we wanted fuel or not we had to stop in line and then we carried on again. And it was getting really, really hairy. The bus couldn't slow down otherwise we reckoned they [the prisoners] would have been off it.

My mate, Colin, says, 'I'll sort this out.' So Colin used to do a stand-up routine, Tommy Cooper, and he gave them half an hour of Tommy Cooper. It was absolutely unbelievable, he made them clear the backseat, and he stood at the back of the bus. I'd got some prisoner next to me, I'd got my stick up my sleeve, and Colin were going [Tommy Cooper impression] and it was absolutely incredible. He got a standing ovation and he did two encores and then we went into Winston Green in Birmingham. It was absolutely magnificent!

As a seasoned officer and then, impressively, governor, of course we also had to get Vanessa's take on what the main sources of disputes between officers and prisoners actually are. We wanted to know what tended to drive conflicts between one prisoner and another, too. She had a ready response to the latter:

'Between prisoners: contraband, drugs, debtors, creditors and trying to "collect debts", bullying, victimisation, minimising offences.'

One prisoner had also indicated to us that things could kick off for a myriad of reasons, although all roads tended to lead back to a celebrity prisoner and other prisoners wanting to look big:

John Worboys [JW] I also know very well. I first met him at HMP Belmarsh. While he was on remand he would maintain his innocence and constantly ask me questions about DNA. He never gave any details of his offending. I was convicted and left Belmarsh and went to HMP W. One afternoon, after JW was convicted, he turned up on my wing, C wing at HMP W. He came on the same bus as Steve.

Steve Barker had caused the death of Baby P.

JW was terrified and came to me for protection. He turned up at my door with and there was Barker. I told Barker to fuck off! Two hours later Barker was assaulted and beaten outside the servery and removed from C wing and given a job in healthcare where he remained.

Over the coming months JW would become close to me. He had property all over, London, Hertfordshire and a flat in Bournemouth. His victims were suing him for compensation.

JW is a very well-spoken man, polite and liked the gym. He gradually settled in. His confidence was knocked when in 2013 he was assaulted very seriously. He was stabbed, slashed and they tried to strangle him using the TV aerial cable. He managed to crawl under the bed and scream for help. I was using the phone at the time. The phone is directly by the officers' table [the observation table at the end of each landing]. I had to finish my call and tell the officers that JW was being attacked. It was pathetic. One officer ran to his door and removed and extended her batten and shouted at them to stop. They just pushed her out the way and shut the cell door and barricaded it. They did nothing. I had to press the alarm bell. Eventually male officers turned up and forced open the door. JW was taken to hospital and returned four days later. I saw his injuries. His neck was marked with the burn marks from the cable friction. His back was slashed all over with many stitches, his head had stitches and he had a black eye. He lost all ability to ever be confident again.

When I left HMP W, JW would write to me. He told me he was getting out and as such he was not allowed to write to other offenders. He was a category A prisoner and he had been given parole as a category A prisoner, which is rare. I did write back to him and told him to refuse any release and ask for an open prison. We was aware of the public outcry over his release and I knew the justice minister would intervene. I told him if he spent some time in open conditions then the government could never argue he was a danger to the public because he had spent time in open conditions and not absconded. Therefore they had no case to keep him in jail. He ignored my advice and went for release; of course the government now had a strong case to fight it. Releasing him from a high-security prison was a strong case for the government. The police ended up charging him with more offences to keep him in. He was now given a life sentence. He told me he pleaded guilty because he would never get a fair trial. JW was certainly guilty of all his crimes and more.

JW now lives in the healthcare department inside HMP W for his own protection. Because of his profile he is now a huge target while he remains at HMP W. JW is petrified of his own shadow, he is no fighter or hard man, very vulnerable and weak. He was always very polite to others. I no longer write to him.

When it came to prisoners and staff, though, Vanessa had very rarely seen deliberate attacks. Of course, staff do get assaulted, but often it's the result of them getting in the way of a prisoner or separating another altercation. As with John and with our Broadmoor experiences, sometimes these altercations would kick off for the most trivial of reasons.

'We had a riot in Holloway in the dining room over a Christmas pudding.' Vanessa explained that one prisoner felt that someone else had gotten a larger slice and kicked off. The staff tried to separate them and some were hurt.

It's very rare to have a one-on-one situation between prisoner and staff. The most critical, and disgusting, situation that Vanessa recalls is of being 'potted' by a prisoner who was disgruntled as a result of being put on Basic. Basic level is for prisoners who have failed to abide by behaviour principles and are therefore denied the extras and privileges that they might get for good behaviour. Potting is the act of a prisoner throwing shit at a prison officer.

Pete mentioned this revolting practice to us, too. He recalled that they didn't have integral sanitation at the time and Pete would be on duty having to reset the buckets. And prisoners would sometimes bump into each other and start on each other. Whilst trying to break it up, Pete would often have the pot thrown over him and become covered in faeces and urine. That's why, as explained earlier, officers would have changes of clothes so they could be back in ten minutes. 'Hey kid, I'm back!'

We asked Martin about assaults he remembered inside Wakefield. He recalled a Welsh lad. The alarm bell went and when they arrived 'he was absolutely bleeding copiously. Someone had smashed a mug over the back of his head. Blood everywhere.'

He also remembers a 'gypsy' that had gone downstairs to get a new television. 'Was walking downstairs with his old television. From landing to landing – around twenty-two stairs. Small landing with ten stairs or so between threes and fours. Somebody booted him down and he was completely out of it.' He did end up with brain damage. 'When he came back he was very slow and couldn't get thoughts together.'

He recalls a very unusual attack one time in the kitchen. One prisoner had stabbed another. 'They were husband and wife, if you like' – a relationship spat. One of them had gone off with somebody else.

Really bad attacks didn't really happen very often though. When you got one it was really bad but it was rare. Plenty of minor scuffles though. 'Can't remember anybody dying but there were some horrific injuries.' Martin remembers one prisoner, a 'big lad', who had the nasty habit of putting two pounds of sugar in a jug with boiling water and whacking somebody with it. Which is particularly nasty. 'But he got sent somewhere that he didn't wanna go and ended up killing himself.'

There were two assault that were memorable for Pete, for all the wrong reasons.

I remember a prisoner being burnt in a cell in a dormitory. Set on fire, tied up, paper put in around him and set on fire. They had matches. They stuffed paper all in his clothing and all around him and set the paper on fire. He were badly burned, and that was when I were on nights. I was the senior officer on nights and my PO and I had to deal with it. We had to evacuate the wing, which isn't the best thing at night. It was smoke filled… I also remember a prisoner having his throat slit. Cos he was a nonce, albeit Wakefield at the time had changed its role to a sex offender unit. So you had paedophiles and rapists, but rapists were ranked higher than paedophiles, as it was worse to have sex with a child than it was with a woman. This kid who had his throat slit was a paedophile.

Another prisoner assisted his cellmate, who had mental health issues, in committing suicide. 'When I worked in security as a principal officer, I was known as the Grim Reaper because I dealt with all the death,' Pete related. He was charged with involuntary manslaughter – moved from the prison and dealt with by the police and not prison service.

'An officer was severely attacked with a homemade shiv, a blade that he'd made in the workshop, and he'd got out and he attacked this officer. He was really badly assaulted, he was hit that hard with this blade that it severed the muscle away from his shoulder blade, and he were in hospital for a long time. Now that prisoner was removed and taken down the segregation unit.' He went to Leeds, was charged and then committed suicide.

A lot of prisoners build a good relationship with the staff, though. 'You know when they're up and you know when they're down', it is part of jail craft. 'You learn your jail craft, that's your bread and butter.'

Pete used to have to deal with the coroners and the police and organise the bodies to be taken away and liaise with the families. In the case of a natural causes death, Pete would liaise with families to donate any property to the local disabled school. 'A lot of the families didn't want anything to do with the prisoners because they were rapists, paedophiles. They were the black sheep of the family kind of thing.'

As we will see in the next chapter, relationships within prisons, both between staff and prisoners but also between inmates, can come in many different forms.

Chapter 18

Love Behind Bars

Martin went on to make the very interesting observation, one we had not heard from any other contributor, that many prison fights were in effect 'lovers' tiffs'.

'A lot of it is really between couples falling out,' Martin explained. 'Quite a few of them couple up.' Martin remembered a new officer joining the team when he worked at another prison.

'He was very nice but naive. He came running up [to Martin] saying, "There's two lads wrestling in their cells" and this old officer said, "Wrestling? I'll have a look at that" and went to inspect. He came back and said, "Lad, you'll never have children if you think that's wrestling."'

When he first joined the service it was frowned upon, but it came to be that prisoners could be supplied with Durex. 'If you had a bad hospital officer on, he'd try to fob them off with petroleum jelly but they didn't like that.'

One prisoner gave us a fascinating account of what

he saw as sexual grooming taking place at Wakefield, involving prisoner Mark Hobson.

Mark Hobson is another high-profile currently located at HMP W. I know Mark very well and spent years with him on C wing and we worked in the Braille shop. Typing out books into Braille. He is very short and skinny. Maybe 5ft 2. Channel 5 made a documentary on him and it claims he attacked Ian Huntley. He did not, in fact Huntley beat him up in the healthcare department at HMP W where they were both being held because it was unsafe to locate them because of their crimes. Hobson was eventually located on C wing where he remains today. He walks with a bounce and is considered a screw boy. Officers' pet. He tries to be judgmental of others but his own crimes are horrendous. He killed an old couple and raped his partner's [twin] sister then killed her and his partner. He was given a whole life in prison.

Hobson works in the category A Braille shop and is actually very articulate on an educational basis. He is very haggard now and just looks like a skinny little old man. He has been punched and beaten up several times because of his attitude. His family live local to HMP W and he has regular visits. He is [a] nobody who just manipulates officers and grovels to them.

In the course of his TV work, Jonathan had been in contact with a fascinating woman, who wrote to prisoners including Levi Bellfield. Jonathan asked her about any stories she had about Wakefield, or love behind bars. She started out by airing her blunt take on Wakefield.

It's a hell hole, I know that lol, mind you they all are. HMP Frankland is not far behind, just corrupt, it's a disgrace... You should have done one on HMP Frankland, lol, got them all in there, and the whole system is corrupt. But as said I think they all are. Wakefield from what Levi said is much bigger, therefore they got away with more stuff, as not enough staff and really, really long corridors. One female staff member, forget her name now, will come to me, she went round having sex with multiple inmates including Levi, but then she settled down to one and got caught and sacked, it was in the paper. Frankland is smaller wings so can't get away with as much, but still get away with a lot.

In her view, Levi had undergone significant behavioural changes at Frankland.

Levi was moved from Wakefield as he was involved in a fight there, with another inmate, but it was the other inmate who inflicted the injuries and I believe he got done for it, and Levi was moved straight into isolation in Frankland. But they didn't keep him isolated long and he has been quite well behaved in Frankland as regarding fighting etc., he doesn't get involved with fights any more, lol. But prison rules are quite childlike and easy to break. They say their sentence is their punishment, and no further punishment should be given in prison. But couldn't be further from the truth, there is pathetic punishments every day.

Martin seemed to have witnessed less impropriety than this when we asked him about it. 'The relationships were pretty good as a rule.' He recalled an amusing incident from his time at Long Lartin though.

'We had a prisoner called Tommy O'Toole who we ended up calling "two-timing Tommy O'Toole" who unfortunately sent two visiting orders out, one to his wife and one to his girlfriend, who turned up in the gate at the same time.'

Another relevant memory that Martin was able to share from Long Lartin involved 'an armed robber, and he escaped from custody'. He told Martin he wanted to be caught, and he'd cycle up and down outside the police station and nobody ever recognised him. And when he went back to prison he didn't want to see his wife.

He said to her, 'No, go and live your life, I'm gonna be in here for fifteen years.' Within the final eighteen months before release, he corresponded with her again and she still loved him and had remained an honest woman. And he organised his first visit in fourteen years. He was messing about in the gym beforehand; he bent down and hit his head, gave himself a black eye. He said. 'That's bloody typical, haven't seen my wife for nearly fourteen years and I'm gonna meet her with a black eye.'

Within women's prisons such as New Hall, same-sex relationships are commonplace. Female prisoners have also been known to enter into sexual relationships with prison officers. This could be in the form of a bribe, usually for drugs or food.

Jo Taylor, having worked at New Hall and at Wakefield, was able to use this perspective to draw some interesting comparisons. In terms of the issues she was aware of at Wakefield, 'Some officers would give cons things. There were four nurses: and one was having sex with a con in healthcare. There was a guy renting out phones. Three females got nine months. In the end it's for money.'

It was a bit different at New Hall, but sexual favours were still bandied around as prison currency. Some women would also, of course, just want the cash. Jo went into a bit more detail about the demographic:

'At New Hall the majority of women are in for drug offences. Stealing, "grafting" – stealing to order. They get 90-odd quid when they leave the prison service.'

We asked Jo about sexual relationships in both Wakefield and in New Hall. What differences were there between the two institutions?

In New Hall, there were many having 'relationships'. Some are gay so they meet up and have a relationship, and some, who were in relationships, shared a cell as there were double cells. Others were what was called 'jail bent': only gay in prison but not on the outside. It was out there and accepted that relationships went on.

In Wakefield, it happened but was very much behind closed doors. They were given condoms as a form of protection from disease but [it was] certainly not on display like the women. They didn't walk round holding hands like the women did. I think it was more frowned upon with the guys from other guys, but it happened. Probably in the showers or cells with someone on lookout!

As women are much closer in life than men, it was more accepted being gay, and quite a lot of the female staff in New Hall were gay also. There were only a couple of male officers. In Wakefield, there were not as many gay female officers and no male officers that I knew that were 'out'. It's harder in that environment for male staff to be out as gay.

For Pete, there were key differences between the staff at Wakefield and at New Hall: 'There are a lot of good staff at New Hall, but there are also a lot of bad staff.'

One case a few years ago made the headlines, possibly in part because of some of the salacious details that emerged in court. Iain Cocks, an officer at HMP New Hall, was convicted in December 2018 at Leeds Crown Court of two offences of misconduct in a public office and sexual assault. His crimes took place between June 2015 and May 2017. His wife was also employed at New Hall at the time.

The conviction was based in part on a two-year relationship that he had with an inmate that involved sex not just in cells but against a washing machine in the prison laundry room and even in the staff room. He had flirted with another inmate prior to sexually assaulting her in her cell. He also had sex, it emerged at his trial, with a third inmate following her release from prison on licence, in the spare room of his own home (while his wife was working a night shift) and on a waterbed.

Judge Simon Phillips concluded: 'A sentence of immediate imprisonment is inevitable.' Iain Cocks had the opportunity to meet the first inmate he had sexual relations with in 2015, when she was moved onto New Hall's Rivendell wing – 'a unit where prisoners are allowed more freedom'. Presumably this was not the sort of freedom that the prison administration had in mind.

Cocks engaged in inappropriate behaviour with the second inmate when she was moved onto the same wing. Cocks indecently assaulted the woman in her cell by rubbing his groin against her. He stopped when she said to him: 'Don't you think I am vulnerable?'

Similar incidents have taken place at Wakefield prison. In May 2011, an inquiry was held following the suspension of a female prison officer after claims that she had an affair with convicted murderer Leigh Thornhill. He was serving a life sentence for the murder of Corinne Bailey in a frenzied attack with a plank of wood in August 2003; he also conducted a serious assault on another woman, Julie Francis, the same night.

The Prison Service said: 'A member of staff from HMP Wakefield has been suspended pending the outcome of an internal investigation.'

It was given that this female officer would not be named unless the investigation led to serious disciplinary or criminal charges, and given that she never was, presumably following the suspension she was cleared of wrongdoing.

Inappropriate relationships, as we know from Broadmoor as well as Wakefield, do happen from time to time in both psychiatric hospitals and prisons, perhaps more frequently than you would think. Like any workplace, as we discovered from our husband-and-wife contributor team, it can also be a place where legitimate love can flourish, even if it doesn't seem that romantic a setting.

We wanted to know from Lisa how she met her husband Paul at Wakefield.

'I was his manager and I was in a bad marriage; he was in a bad relationship and we worked together and just got to know each other. And twenty-five years later we're still together.'

They didn't let their relationship impact their work. 'He had his job to do, I had my job to do.' Lisa said laughing that Paul was very good at his job, but if he were to have done anything wrong, Lisa would have let him know, no question. They also 'hardly spoke about work' once their workdays were over.

'We'd probably catch up on a bit of gossip or things like that, but we didn't talk about work. Uniform off and that is it.'

This all sounded very harmonious, and it led us to wonder if there was any stigma attached to staff getting together at work? Lisa said, prior to their relationship, there had been other instances of male and female staff getting together, so the idea was not new and there wasn't too much of a stigma around it as maybe in the past. But that wasn't to say there was no judgement entirely.

'Some staff had bets on how long we would stay together. You just had to laugh that off.' Some staff did also tend to spread rumours around. 'That's one thing with Wakefield, Chinese whispers does happen.' Again, this didn't affect their relationship as her and her husband were able to separate the rumours from reality.

When we asked Pete the much broader question about what in his view could be improved in the UK prison service, he framed his response partially in terms of sexual misdeeds. There was the imperative that we put more funding into prisons. 'There's more people resigning than what they're employing.' For him it needs more discipline, too. Without that, sexual issues could arise.

'Young girls going in as officers, male prisoners being overly protective. [That leads] to sexual relations and then trafficking drugs and contraband into the prison: conditioning of officers.'

Given the possibility that these events can take place though, it is hard not to speculate that there must be many other affairs, both between fellow prisoners and between prisoners and prison workers, that never come to light. Several of our contributors did not wish to go on record about this but assured us that they were aware of sexual stories that were not in the public domain.

When these relationships are non-consensual and

abusive, they can have a terrible effect on prisoners' mental health, leading to increased trauma and self-harm. It was something we wanted to place in the bigger picture of the path to rehabilitation and mental health for prisoners.

Chapter 19

Prisoner Rehabilitation and Mental Health

As always, John Hartstone could be relied upon to give a fascinating, balanced and compassionate account. When asked about perceptions surrounding prisoners and whether any prisoners were not as he expected, with an insight that was both knowledgeable and philosophical, John stated: 'A murderer is only a murderer for about five minutes of their lives.'

This begs the question: 'Is it right that we treat people or label people for something that they've done for five minutes of their lives? Probably not.'

In his view, perceptions of prisoners, particularly murderers, are often warped. For professionals like John who have spent so much time with them in their daily professional life, in many ways they are just like regular people.

'They all enjoy a bit of company, they're all talking about the last film they saw, the last book they've read, what's on television. What they're interested in, what they're not interested in. There are subjects that you'd want to avoid when speaking to them, but generally speaking, if you treat them other than ordinary people, they're going to pick up on it and you're looking at problems.'

When we asked John to reflect on the most rewarding part of his career, he explained that from the early 1990s, he was heavily involved in the national sex offender treatment programme (SOTP). Though rewarding, it was also, understandably, extremely challenging.

The programme focused on an exploration of the use of detailed interview techniques that could then be used to help to reduce the offending behaviour of sex offenders. In the case of sex offenders, according to John, often a court won't have the full picture of the crime: namely the motivation and reasoning behind such offences.

'If you don't understand what you've done and why you've done it, how the hell are you supposed to avoid it in the next phase?'

Therefore, the idea was to uncover, through intense and detailed interviewing techniques, what exactly occurred at the time of the offence, why it happened, and how to try and avoid it in the future.

Whilst the programme was overall a rewarding experience, and John was able to work with a multitude of specialisms and gain vital understanding of different prison roles, he described his work with the sex offender treatment programme as 'extremely traumatising. To the point where two of my colleagues took their own lives.'

The intensity of having to interact and engage with such dark and traumatic material proved too much. Counselling was introduced for some of the course facilitators to help with the mental strain, though this was introduced as John was moving away from that area, so he didn't really experience or benefit from that innovation.

The striking analogy that John deployed in this context was to compare his work in the programme to giving blood. He confessed that he doesn't like needles. Even so, he has given blood for many years: 'I believe if a person has an ability to do something, and it causes them a little bit of upset, if it's worth doing then it should be done. If you can possibly do it, then you should do it.'

Whilst the programme was used to help prisoners to rehabilitate themselves, it also gave John valuable interviewing skills that he could apply to his role as a prison officer. In another prison, John recalled to us a time that he had been called to investigate the death of an inmate. As we note elsewhere in this book, this is normally a traumatic event, and one that has a rigorous, formal process attached to it.

After interviewing a prisoner using the methods that John was taught to use on the programme, he was able to uncover the truth. The prisoner disclosed that he had been involved in the inmate's death. Whilst unpleasant, such skills were useful to have.

The programme also exposed John to people from lots of different specialisms where he could gain understanding and appreciation of their impact on prisoners. He worked very closely with probation and psychology, meaning he was able to appreciate their contributions to prisoner life. As John was to explain, experiences of prisoners can be very different across specialisms.

One of the more controversial topics encountered in John's career was discussion around prisoner-patient management. John explained that one of the recurring issues arises when officers become overly familiar with prisoners and take risks with their management. For example, if a current prisoner shows similarities to another inmate who had been previously rehabilitated, officers or other professionals may compare the progress of the two and take risks with the current inmate.

This can have the very unwanted consequence of potentially putting either staff or prisoners at risk. Part of these risks come from a certain division between roles within a prison. Different roles are subject to different experiences with prisoners, and they are less inclined to listen: 'Not only do they not understand the perspective that you're coming from, but they don't appreciate it because they can't relate to it.'

These kinds of miscommunications allow for risks that are otherwise avoidable. In John's experience, there is a culture of deference. Degree-educated people who work in prisons – such as psychologists and probationary workers – are able to articulate their thoughts in a more 'educated and articulate' way that higher-ups are more likely to listen to.

So, prisoner reports can often be biased, because

psychiatrist reports and more formal documents are more likely to be taken into account rather than those of prison officers, who may not be able to express their experiences in the same articulate way. It can be a big loss to suppress these diverse views with what is effectively unconscious bias because even if the officer's experience is significantly different to the educated professional's, their expertise could be equally or even more valuable.

This often innate 'snobbery' within the system also transfers to matters of the parole process. John notes that then Home Secretary Dominic Raab had recently announced that the parole process for prisoners was changing, as decisions were often weighed too heavily on specialists who don't interact with prisoners on a regular basis.

As John succinctly describes it: 'When you've been locked up twenty, twenty-five years, and you go see the psychology department every fortnight, and probation every week, you absolutely understand all the buzz words, you absolutely understand how to present yourself. You understand all that. The thing about it is, while you're presenting in one way, you can't possibly present that way all your life, if it ain't you. You get an imbalance of views then.'

John then emphasised that the viewpoints of prison officers and those working on the wings regularly should have more weight behind parole decisions, even if their descriptions may not be as eloquent or use as many specialist phrases. Or jargon, if we are being unkind.

John, having worked alongside a multitude of roles and job titles, is privileged enough to understand how the system works, and has taken it upon himself to advocate for and against people based on his experiences, to make patient decisions as fair as possible.

* * *

Having started his prison career at twenty-one years old, Wakefield was the first prison 'Jim' ever visited, and the appearance of Wakefield was a stark comparison to its reality:

'[There] were fairly forbidding walls, painted a bright colour so the cameras could see anybody against them... It looked pretty scary, it's obviously a proper prison, it looks like an impressive prison. But actually, inside the buildings, it had quite a relaxed atmosphere, the prisoners and staff plainly getting on well actually. And staff having an obvious understanding of their prisoners.

Jim believes that this deep understanding by Wakefield staff of its prisoners is what sets the prison apart from other high-security institutions. Having looked after high-security prisoners, mainly murderers, it knows how to do it; people learn from one another. 'There's a deep understanding of what it's like to do a long-term sentence and how you might get people through it.'

In his time there, there was a very limited staff turnover. They got to know both the job and the prisoners very well. As part of his role, Jim assessed prisoner wellbeing, and issues such as whether there were drugs being snuck into the prison, or if prisoners had access to things they were entitled to, such as clean clothes and phone calls.

As a very significant contribution to mental health, Lisa was one of the people who brought in the 'listeners scheme' to Wakefield, she believes in the late 1990s, and trained the prisoners up for it.

'There's a lot of things prisoners don't want to talk to staff about, which is fine. And there's a lot of things that if they did talk to us about, we probably wouldn't fully understand. So, to get a fellow prisoner who understands totally what that prisoner's going through, and using the same language, the same jargon, the same whatever, if it helps that prisoner that's in crisis? Fantastic.'

The prisoners chosen as listeners were vetted and they underwent a training course for it. They were fully supported by chaplaincy and the psychology department so that they could offload as well if needed. The training process for listeners involved developing counselling skills. It also involved outlining what limitations the listeners have. If the situation becomes more than the listener can handle, that would be relayed to the upper management. Then the prisoner would either be directed to more professional help, such as a psychiatrist, or they would get a different listener in.

'Some listeners could be in with a prisoner that's in crisis all night and not being able to sleep, and all day. Until that prisoner feels okay, that he can cope, then that listener will stay with him. So they do an absolutely fantastic job.'

When it comes to criteria for selecting prisoners, Lisa

told us that the type of crime committed didn't affect their ability to become listeners. The length of their sentences also didn't matter. It was just based on how they behaved – they were recommended by staff and vetted, very specially chosen. The only ones who weren't allowed to apply to be a listener were the category A prisoners.

We had amazing first-hand prisoner testimony about being a listener, too, thanks to Jenny who had been trained to do it on a voluntary basis by the Samaritans charity when she was a prisoner.

We'd go on shift. Around eight of us for the whole prison. Not a lot of people wanted to do it. If a paedophile wanted to talk to you then you would have to go and listen to them. If somebody was struggling a listener would go into their cell and speak to them. It was one on one and confidential. Even if they told listeners they were going to kill themselves, they weren't allowed to tell anyone. The only exception was if they were planning to commit an act of terrorism. If the officers asked if they were alright or not they had to say 'You know you can't ask me that.'

They had one in the day and two on shift at night. They could be called out at 3am. Some girls would say they needed a listener to get access to hot water. They would then get locked away again. Sometimes girls would say they could not cope, and were planning to self-harm.

When Jenny went to the healthcare wing as a listener,

the guards would say 'stand back, don't stand near the doors' as shit would be thrown through there; they would try and grab and hurt you. That felt like she was walking through Broadmoor and she understandably found it 'really creepy'.

* * *

The wonderful Hayley Grocock is another contributor whose work has brought her into contact with prisoner rehabilitation at Wakefield Prison, in her role as Chief Executive of Wakefield District Sight Aid. When she took on the role in September 2017, she was soon made aware of something that she found utterly extraordinary and intriguing.

'I had never worked with people with sight loss before. We have 1200 members of blind and partially sighted people across the district of Wakefield. I was told that the Braille materials were produced at Wakefield Prison. I said, "How does that work?" I had never heard of that! I could not get my head around it.'

It was news to us, too and we could not wait to learn more about it. Hayley gave us a bit of background.

'In history, quite a lot of prisons had Braille units. It was seen as part of the rehabilitation process. Only two prisons still have Braille units [Wakefield is one of them]. The staff team at Wakefield is three, maybe four of them, they are former prison officers.'

We wanted to know all about the unit when she visited it a couple of years ago.

'There were no men working in the unit when I went because of an IT issue, all the computers were stacked up against the back of the room.'

It turned out that there had been an IT breach, which had put the existence of the Braille unit into jeopardy. 'The future of the Braille unit looked dicey because the governor thought after the IT breach it was more trouble than it was worth.'

Of course, Hayley explained, other places offer Braille transcription services: but they charge you for doing it. Wakefield was performing a genuine public service for free. As she looked around the Braille unit, Hayley found it an emotional and inspiring experience.

'The impact of being there... On the walls there were letters, cards, notes of thanks from blind people. There was a thank you card from a blind schoolgirl. They had transcribed all her educational resources for her whole school career. All the certificates too. A lot of the men have little to no qualifications at all, but these Wakefield prisoners are trained to produce this incredibly complicated Braille.'

Hayley was overwhelmed by the work that was being done and the contribution it made, and was fearful that one of these only two remaining last bastions could go under.

'I wrote a letter to the number one governor of the prison saying, "Don't close the Braille unit: it's so important." I wrote a letter once a year describing the positive impact of the prison's Braille work on my stakeholders.'

An intelligent and humane person, Hayley could see

that there had to be a positive impact for the Wakefield prisoners doing the work as well as for her service users. 'I can't ever subscribe to the view that anybody is beyond redemption. There but for the grace of God. Give someone the opportunity to be proud of something.'

She continued: 'There is a big asylum seeker house next to the prison in Wakefield. The thing that is removed in all of these situations is hope. The letters, cards and certificates I saw that the men had achieved. It gives them hope, it gives them purpose. If you take that away from people, that is inhumane.'

Hayley recalled another case in which a service user had bought a new microwave and phoned the manufacturer and asked for the instructions in Braille. Cruelly, the manufacturer said no. They sent it to the Wakefield Braille unit, they did it and sent it back. This made a world of difference to someone who wanted to lead a normal life. Hayley summed up her feelings on Wakefield prisoner rehabilitation in memorable terms.

I had never been in a high-security prison before. Be under no illusion that in this room will sit some of the baddest bastards to ever walk the earth, but when they come into this room, maybe for the first time in their life, they feel useful. A lot of these men are never getting out, but they can go into a room and learn a very specialist skill – and that has a transformative effect on some of the baddest bastards in the world.

Our prisoner would corroborate Hayley's description here, describing the type of characters working in the Braille shop in the following terms:

I worked in the Braille shop, it was a mini monster house. Bellfield, Mark Hobson, Colin Ireland ['Gay Slayer' serial killer from London in the 1980s], Robert Black [serial child killer], Peter Moore [Welsh serial killer of gay men in the 1980s], Mike Little [murdered a girl on her way home and kept the body and raped her corpse until she was found in his shed], John Worboys ['Black Cab Rapist', now goes by the name of John Radford]. Colin Ireland died some years ago. He went out to hospital for a routine operation and died later from a blood clot. Colin I knew very well and was close to. He was located on B wing and very funny. Always telling jokes. He was 6ft 3 but a gentle giant. He would always joke with Worboys, saying the revolution was coming and they would soon be free. He always would joke that when they were free they'd go on a killing spree and Worboys would be his driver. Colin would go on about killing more gay men. Colin had serious gum disease and his breath absolutely stunk, it was brutal. He hated Robert Black and they never spoke.

Our contributor Martin recalled Robert Black in more complimentary terms than our prisoner: 'very polite, just got on with it'.

Pete also described him to us. 'Robert Black was on

twos, he was a very quiet man. Very evil looking man. And he used to look at you, but not say anything, before he'd ask for general things that other prisoners would ask for. He was escorted everywhere, and searched every few weeks.'

Pete worked in collaboration with the police for a little while. They wanted to break Robert Black down to get information out of him in relation to other crimes.

'They reckon that there were a lot of kids that he killed, that the poor families never found out where their children were buried. That's perhaps why I didn't think too much about it, because if you sat and thought about him, and the crimes that he'd committed, it would be so difficult to actually interact with him and live as well. Because you have flashbacks about these people.'

One prisoner described Robert Black being absolutely loathed in Wakefield by most.

Robert Black was located on D wing. He was a short man who had a bald head and wore glasses. He would visit Whiting's cell and he was hated by many. A soft Scottish accent, he would just walk with his head down. In a strange way he was never really attacked. He was a little overweight and had heart issues.

I told him never to speak to me in the Braille shop. There was times when he would have to come to my desk to give me a book to proofread in Braille. Me, Colin Ireland and Hobson had little sticky notes on our desks. If Black needed anything he was told to write it down on

*the sticky note pad and that is how we communicated.
He eventually went to Ireland to face justice and was
convicted. As reported, he died in prison in Ireland of
natural causes.*

Although not mentioned in this context by our prisoners,
Jeremy Bamber has also been active in the Braille room
at HMP Wakefield. In fact, he has won several awards
for transcribing books in the prison's Braille workshop.
He has also during his long tenure there worked as a peer
partner, helping other illiterate or semi-literate prisoners
to learn to read and write.

It came as no surprise that our contributor Jim had
a typically well-informed and stimulating perspective
on prisoner welfare and rehabilitation. He expressed
passionately how the notoriety and publicity of Wakefield
affected his work. He described his job as being made
harder by speculation by the media on prison operations,
noting that politicians and the media often became
preoccupied with glorifying prisons or rumouring that
they were 'holiday camps'. As he firmly noted: 'They are
not holiday camps. They never were. They probably feel
tougher at the moment than they have for some time.'

Indeed, he expressed disdain for the media perpetuating
stories of Monster Mansion, noting that spreading such
harmful stories and creating this harmful stigma can make
the rehabilitation of prisoners into the outside world more
difficult. Even so, Jim concluded that he enjoyed his
time working in high-security prisons such as Wakefield.

We found this particularly admirable given that the quality of care for staff has been as inconsistent as that towards patients in the past.

Vanessa was partially drawn into prison work by her idealism. 'I have always been interested in true crime; the prison service happened by accident... I like to be fuelled by challenges.'

If she could help one prisoner it would be worthwhile. 'When someone says, "You won't see me back again, gov" and you don't, and you hear that they've got a job and they've got a place to live and their family has moved back in with them, and they're doing well, you think "Yeah, good". What more satisfaction can you have?'

Yes, there is potentially great satisfaction to be had, but we learned all about the toll it can take on staff, too.

Chapter 20

Staff Care

The world of violent crime is a tough one for anyone to step into. Of course, unlike the devastated families and friends who are thrust into the world by a terrible crime against a loved one, crime writers enter it voluntarily. Even so, as we stated in our introduction, it can take its toll. Sleepless nights, racing to your car and home at night, holding your children closer in fear. With such a long, varied and illustrious career, we asked true-crime writer Geoffrey what had stayed with him the most. He has dealt with so many notorious and haunting cases that he found it hard to pick just one.

'The random cases stick in my mind. They really get to me. They haunt me. Take Dale Cregan. That always sticks in my mind because it was a deliberate decision to kill two police officers. It's utterly horrifying. David Bieber too... there are some random killings that don't come from anywhere comprehensible. It slightly takes your breath away.'

For staff, every single former officer that we spoke to had needed to develop strategies of self-preservation. We asked Vanessa how she managed to emotionally detach herself during the most stressful situations. 'That is very difficult.' When she left the prison service, she actually suffered from post-traumatic stress disorder (PTSD) symptoms. 'Because you compartmentalise everything that's gone on and you desensitise from it.'

It was clear from talking to Vanessa that when you see so many horrific things, things a 'normal job' would never expose you to, you have to put it in the back of your mind and not think about it. She recalled one of the most difficult to deal with experiences that she had.

'There was one prisoner who I really sort of struggled with... [she mentioned that his name is in the public domain but did not give it]. He murdered his girlfriend after a drug-fuelled evening... he literally ruptured her insides with his fists and left her there to bleed, and his mother covered it up, or tried to cover it up for him.'

During his trial and subsequently, he had blamed it on the drugs, but Vanessa noted that he had previous records of abusive behaviour towards women, such as flashing.

She describes what happened to the woman as 'horrendous'. She felt for the victim and how much she would have suffered. 'And he used to waltz around the wing like nothing happened.'

She had to reply to him as you would anyone else and

engage with him whilst being aware of what he had done. She had to write a report on him.

'I wanted to write how absolutely horrendous he was, but actually what I ended up writing was "A is doing very well, he's adapted to the regime of D wing, he's got involved with the gymnasium", that sort of thing, but really that's not what I wanted to write. But that's the whole point, isn't it?'

Sometime those repressed memories have to come to the surface to be processed. For Vanessa, this was when she retired and wrote a book about her experiences. She found it both cathartic but also difficult to go through some of those memories.

What it did teach her was that it's okay not to be okay. She observed that the prison service has a tendency not to properly check in with prison staff after an incident below a surface level 'you alright?' and then you move on. She could never sit down and talk things through, there was no proper aftercare. Unfortunately, this is a familiar story to us, from both historic accounts by Wakefield staff and from many of the close protection officers that we met. For these brave, dedicated women and men, the mental health support, even after the most traumatic of incidents, was simply not there.

What support was there for prison workers, and was it effective? When Vanessa left the prison service, they were coming around to the idea of proper debriefs for staff after an incident to check in with workers. But not whilst she was there. She still thinks there's much more to be done to support prison workers. They've cut back the training to six weeks and it only happens at the jail concerned. They need longer and more varied training. Vanessa did a college course instead to help train for it. She wanted to ensure that she would get a more well-rounded experience. 'On-the-job training to me is a cop out.'

As she pointed out, you have to teach workers interpersonal skills, diversity issues, corruption prevention and so on when they could be doing their job. If you have to teach someone who has no experience, then it's not as effective as it could be. All her experience indicates that it is better to learn these skills away from the prison, with people who have the time to teach properly, rather than on the job.

Fundamentally, she sees the justice system as out of date.

'If you have someone who comes into prison short term – for example, three months – you can't really do much in that time, but that person will probably lose his job, lose his family, lose his relationship and reputation, and once he leaves he will have gained experience in how to commit crimes from other prisoners, and who does that help? He is then more likely to reoffend.'

Vanessa does not want tax money to go towards prison places; she would rather the money went towards rehabilitation and cutting crime, and education. Education of young people and what happens in prison: she sees these as significant preventative methods. 'Eighty per cent of prisoners can't read or write. There has to be more of a move towards educating people. Many prisoners' issues, such as addiction, or homelessness, are social issues, and it's these that we need to target.

'We have the worst reoffending rates in the rest of Europe, so what does that say to you? Something I get asked all the time is "Does prison work?" At the moment, no.'

She is very passionate about this.

'Prison is not a vote winner. Nobody wants to vote for the party that's going to invest in reducing reoffending, to invest in reoffending programmes for prisoners. Norway completely turned itself on its head and it focused on reducing reoffending and not locking prisoners up, and they've got one of the best rates of non-reoffending in Europe.'

Just like Jim though, Vanessa is able to look back with pride on her achievements as well as reflect on how the support system could be better. Having shared some of the lowlights of her career, we wanted to hear a highlight from her, too.

The day I got the notice that I'd got an MBE. Nobody in my family had ever received such recognition or an honour like that. I had a difficult start in life and I proved a lot of people wrong. That's what the honours should be for – it should be for people out in communities making real change. The day I was there, there were a lot of charity workers. It was very humbling. To me, I'd just done my job, I hadn't done anything special.

In our second meeting, Vanessa contemplated the misogyny and homophobia that she had also, unfortunately, encountered at times during her illustrious career. We talked more generally about her experience of being a woman in the traditionally very male world of prison officers in men's prisons. Vanessa started her career in a female prison, which was already full of women officers. Cross-postings came in around 1988 for her when she had already been in the job for two years. She went to Wormwood Scrubs.

> *I think that as a woman you have to earn your stripes. It's very difficult for women to walk in and have the same respect as a man. Most of them [the male officers] were very good and some were very mindful of everything they said, their Ps and Qs, when they were around me until they got to know me. Even prisoners, quite often I'd have a prisoner say to another prisoner, 'Don't say that in front of miss, she don't need to hear that sort of language.' A lot of men are very protective of women: regardless if they work with them or are prisoners.*

Vanessa went on to say that she heard more homophobic and racist jokes when she went to Wormwood Scrubs than she ever did at Holloway. 'You can say, well that's male banter, and we all know that it happens. I'm not saying that it's right because it's not, but it does happen and it probably still does today. That is the nature of the beast.

As a woman you do have to work that little bit harder to gain that respect whereas it comes to men easier.'

Particularly at the Scrubs, quite a lot was put on her because she was a woman. Not necessarily negatively, she explained, but because they thought her communication skills as a woman would be better. In one instance, she was asked to bring in a new structure on D wing and had to take all staff and go through the system. There were three SOs in charge: her and two males. They asked Vanessa to present it as they thought it'd be better coming from a woman. She was happy to do it.

There was the occasional undermining comment. She doesn't want that side of things to be the focus of her work, though; she describes it as miniscule in comparison to the good. She did face homophobia. She was called a dyke quite a lot – 'she only got the job because she's a dyke' – and was often defined by her sexuality.

She felt that was unfair as she wouldn't judge someone like that in the same way, it was immaterial to her work, which speaks for itself. Looking back, it's not what she focuses on; she likes to focus on the positives of her career. She has clearly been through a lot but remains optimistic about the profession and most of her peers.

Another of our female contributors, Lisa, was able to really enrich this narrative for us, when we asked her how prisoners treated her.

The majority of the prisoners I would say were absolutely fantastic, they were really good. Some of them had been in prison for such a long time that they hadn't had that female contact. I was always well aware of what some of the prisoners were in there for. You were always aware of that. Some of the prisoners in there have got a deep hatred towards females, that's why they've committed the crime and that's why they're in prison. But on the whole, prisoners wanted to come out and talk to you about the wife, about the girlfriend, their children, show you photographs, have that female contact. And with us as a group, the female staff tended to help with that 'you don't have to be macho anymore' calming influence.

As far as Lisa is aware, there were no policies at the time to help to protect female staff from sexism in the workplace. There might have been, but the staff at Wakefield were never aware of them.

Of course, it is certainly not just female prison staff who were made to feel vulnerable, and we wanted to ask Pete all about his experiences in this context, too. What had struck him the most about mental health and support for staff?

'Years ago, there was nothing, [it was] absolute garbage. It were, "Get on with it lad, it happens, this is jail."'

Pete's memories extend back to the late 1980s, when he recalls that mental health was downplayed. 'This is the jail service, not kindergarten!'

Even assaults on staff were minimised and patronised on occasions, dismissed out of hand. 'You've only had a smack, that's not a bad assault.'

Nowadays things have changed. There is counselling available for staff.

Going back to Lisa, she was involved with the sex offender treatment programme (SOTP), and we wanted to know what it was like, as a woman, to deal with people who were sex offenders. 'You have to be very professional.'

It was a fifty-two-week programme, involving prisoners being challenged on their offences. 'I knew every minute detail of their offence. I saw photographs of victims, I saw not very nice things and was talking regarding children and stuff like that. But you have to be professional.'

Some staff were not able to deal with the dreadful stress of working the SOTP. One colleague committed suicide because of it; they were Paul's friend. For Lisa, somehow, she said, 'you have to come home and switch that off.'

What if that's not possible? 'Some people can do it. Sadly, some people can't. And if you can't then really you cannot become a prison officer because it is a hard job. It's a job done behind walls that people can't see.'

Our contributor Jo had a very different and characteristically hilarious take on the programme!

The sex offenders' programme: what a load of shite that is, in my opinion! Say you were in a prison and they said, 'You want to have sex with a man, or with a woman, but no, you have to have sex with an animal', it's like, 'I don't want to.' But if I follow all this stuff and tick all the boxes, I will get out and go back to what I think is normal. They'll tick all the boxes and say, 'Oh

287

yeah, I'm a paedophile, shouldn't be doing it with babies and toddlers'... to get the ticks. 'Oh yes, I'm reformed now. Done all the courses! I can see what I did was wrong.' What does he do when he gets out? Goes back to what he thinks is normal. 'How the fucking hell... I do believe they are all together in a room like Alcoholics Anonymous. What are they doing? They're learning new things from the others! It's like 'Oh, God, I hadn't thought of that! I'll do that when I get out!'

Pete was also involved in the programme. He was a tutor. It was a very difficult experience for him: reliving the crimes of the prisoners and talking them through it, and roleplaying different scenarios of the victim, of the perpetrator.

Pete worked with an officer, from Barnsley, who committed suicide as a result of the programme. After that, they introduced counselling for the officers; it was mandatory when working on the SOTP. Pete went and didn't find it helpful, he simply said that he always felt 'fine' when the counsellor asked.

'I could separate work and home. And I didn't have a problem with that. Work I saw as "bad things happen at work" but as soon as I leave those gates, I'm then Pete Wightman, the family man.'

Pete told us that he never spoke about work at home or things that had happened. He didn't want his young daughters to hear. 'When I went to work, I put it on, I was a prison officer, when I took it off, I was a family man.'

'And when I'd meet people who'd say "I can't believe you work at Wakey prison", to me it's just like working in a factory, you go in the morning, you clock on, you do your job, you clock off, you come home. That's the way I did it.'

As he continued: 'I've been retired five years now. You do dwell on things, you do live and breathe it. And when you have serious incidents, you do get flashbacks. I still do occasionally now have dreams about work and things that have happened, and it is hard to deal with at times. You've got to be a strong character to work in the service… You become institutionalised and it's difficult to get out of that pattern.'

The sadness of working in an environment like HMP Wakefield can accumulate over the years. 'I have lost a lot of colleagues from Wakefield in the last twenty-five years. Sadly, we're losing even more recently.'

We knew that there would be many good memories too, though, and wanted to know what parts of his Wakefield employment he had enjoyed the most. He immediately responded that it was the 'camaraderie'.

People talk to you about prison banter: there's nothing like it. Prison officers have a weird sense of humour, and you need it, you need it to cope with all the crap that you see. They will laugh at things that you think, 'Oh my god that's so inappropriate', because they're dealing with that much shit. It's not every day that you can say you've worked with someone like Robert Black, who's killed multiple children.

The support from fellow officers was the primary mental support at the time, before there was any other proper form of support.

Lisa gave us a lively description of banter, too, stating, 'I love the banter between staff.' She told us that staff would have nicknames for each other. 'It's a coping mechanism, where you kind of take the mickey out of each other. It's not done seriously. That's just a coping mechanism to keep them smiling, to get people laughing.'

Lisa got called 'Tina' at one time because she smoked and was called 'Nico-Tina' but otherwise didn't really have a nickname.

'We had one officer who was in the army for a long time, in fact he were quite high-ranking in the army, and he lived in Durkar in Wakefield and he was called the "Durkar Gurkha". It suited him... My husband is quite good at English and things like that and quite clever, so he got the nickname "Prof".'

Returning to Pete, he had more to say on the support network on offer.

'In those days people generally worked locally. So you worked and lived together – staff lived in quarters, so they had prison officers' clubs, so they'd finish work, half past nine on a night, they'd go home, have a bit of supper, and then go over to the club and have a few beers together, and that's the way that you relieved that pressure.'

Many of our contributors were keen to stress, implicitly or explicitly, that this was not a career you went into for the money, either. As Pete said to us:

'People think that prison officers were rich people. They weren't.'

Pete recalls how he missed his daughters growing up because he had been working so many hours to pay the mortgage. Many took the option of overtime to get more money, even though the pay wasn't that great. He had a wry recollection about his work ethic during this period of his life.

'They used to call me "Martini Man" at one time. Any time, any place, anywhere. Because I'd do any overtime, I'd do bed watches, I'd do escorts, all to get extra money to put food on the table and educate my children. A hell of a lot of officers used to do the same.'

Sadly, it was not surprising to learn in this context that substance misuse is a genuine and common problem, and Pete worked with a lot of alcoholics in his time as an officer.

'What they used to say was, the majority of prison officers retired at fifty-five and were dead by sixty, because they worked that many hours, they smoked like chimneys and drank like fish, because that's how they dealt with all the stress and pressure.'

We knew that Martin would offer his characteristically humane and humorous take on his survival methods for distancing himself emotionally from the job too. 'Easy. I never looked at what they'd done. I didn't let anything influence me, I dealt with everybody as they were on that day.'

In his view, because sex offenders generally exhibit a

protracted, thought-out process of long-term grooming, not by accident, they very rarely would want to talk about what they'd done. And Martin wouldn't ask. In the same vein, Martin's response when he chose a rapist for his rugby team in a game at HMP Long Lartin was: 'I'm not here to judge him, I'm here to look after him. The punishment is loss of liberty.'

Even so, despite putting up his best defences, Martin realised about three months before retirement that he was suffering from PTSD, 'from all the things I'd seen'. He shared the striking memory that when searching cells, 'people will have a box with pictures of their crime and you can't help when you're looking through them and you're seeing it.'

Things like that started to get on top of him. 'I realised my time was coming where I wasn't going to stay much longer in the service.'

This is why he reverted back to being an SO and worked on the gate later in his career. It was critical for his mental well-being.

'Quite a lot of people suffer PTSD and a lot of them don't realise they've got it. But you can see it, because you can see the haunting in the eyes and you can just see that it's got to them. It's just like a paramedic, a paramedic can go to 150 accidents, the 160th knocks them straight off their feet. And it's the same with prison officers.'

Of course, we wanted to know what that critical tipping point was for him.

I was acting governor at the time and there was a prisoner and he was on adjudication and he wouldn't go to the segregation unit. So, we did the adjudication at his cell door, and basically I was just going to open the cage and he could then get legal representation. And he started cutting his arms in front of me. I felt myself swoon, I felt myself feel sick and my head started to go. And then I pulled myself together, rigidly disciplined my body not to do anything. Nobody would have known that. Nobody saw that, nobody had any idea. But I knew it. I felt it. And I knew... like a marathon runner I was going to start to hit the wall.

This unsettling, nauseating experience was distressing to even hear about from such a committed member of staff, and we were keen to learn about the support he received from the service in the wake of it.

They had counselling, but very, very few people would admit to stress. Because stress had a bit of a stigma about it. It shouldn't have done, but it did. So, if you went sick with stress, [people would comment] 'Gah, he just can't cope with the job! Useless.' Which isn't a fact, anybody can suffer from it... I got offered counselling, but because I was an ex-serviceman and I'd seen quite horrific things in that time, I knew how to deal with it and come out the other side and suppress it.

Martin had other shocking stories. He used to work in the care team looking after other staff. He got a phone call one day from an officer who said he was on the top of the multi-storey car park in Wakefield about to throw himself off. Martin was able to get him help but it left him shaky for months, that someone could get that bad and nobody knew about it until it was almost too late. '[Being] also in the care team looking after staff, and that had an inherent stress level that nobody saw, that shook me to the core.'

Plus, of course, normal life goes on. People were also often suffering with issues at home, their marriages and children, and people like Martin on the care team also found themselves embracing this additional stress. 'Just because you're a prison officer doesn't mean you're not part of the normal society that's happening around you.'

Martin remembers an officer said to him once, 'When you're a manager, you come to work with problems, and if your workers come to work with a problem: he's got a problem and you've got a problem.' In other words, the 'higher-ups' take on the stresses of their workers to help them. Often people who don't seek help become difficult to work with and they make silly mistakes.

You wonder sometimes if they're doing it on purpose because they want someone to notice. People don't like admitting that they've got weaknesses. Which is understandable, because prisoners spend their whole time looking for a weakness. If they find a weakness in a member of staff, then that means they can work on that weakness and use it to their advantage. So what you've gotta do is have no weakness – but none of us have no weakness.

In order to change these macho perceptions that many workers had, you had to change people's perceptions, and Martin had realised that Wakefield didn't like change.

'Wakefield didn't change easily; it was like a big elephant that thought it was doing everything right when it wasn't doing anything right.'

He described what he interpreted as a painful process of Wakefield: 'Having to open up and find that it [Wakefield] wasn't as good as it thought it was and – shock of shocks – that that was because people had never been anywhere else so they'd seen what they'd seen and thought it was the only way to do it.'

People were attached to old ways of thinking. When Martin joined they didn't even have a care team. Previous generations were not encouraged to open up about mental health but rather to keep quiet, so this new concept seemed alien.

So, taking all this on board, what would Martin want to improve for prison workers? He immediately had a few specifics.

'Promotion needs taking out of local hands: not always promoting internally and potentially being biased. [That can lead to] having people ascend higher than they are qualified and ensuring people don't get well-rounded experiences other than in one prison. They [need to] experience different ways of doing things.'

Martin summarised: 'In general the staff was good at Wakefield.' But he did note an odd dichotomy. 'If you don't have problems with prisoners, then you have problems with staff.'

He gave an example from Long Lartin, where there were plenty of alarm bells going off and the staff had to constantly pull together. At Wakefield when you have 'no common enemy' (ex-Marine's terminology) and the prisoners are behaving and everything runs smoothly, then 'the staff will nitpick with each other'.

* * *

Did our contributor Pete have similar experiences and conclusions? Pete actually raised something with wide-ranging implications for staff and prisoner welfare: the introduction of mandatory DNA testing for convicted prisoners. In 1995, the United Kingdom National DNA Database (NDNAD) was founded by the National Policing Improvement Agency (NPIA) as a way of logging DNA samples from criminal suspects.

At the time, Pete was a security PO and he was involved in this. There was a special task unit from the police who came into Wakefield and took the DNA of over 100 prisoners. People were getting caught for crimes they committed decades earlier because DNA testing wasn't available at the time. But their time had finally run out.

The crime it solved was the appalling fate of the 'Babes

in the Wood'. A Wakefield inmate, Ronald Jebson, was found out through DNA testing at Wakefield Prison.

He killed one of these children, the 'Babes in the Wood', and he was found out when they made DNA testing mandatory. Because a lot of the older ones, when they were arrested, DNA testing weren't in.

He actually admitted to the crime and took the police down London to the place where he buried this young lass years ago. So that were like 'Yes!' you know? That were a win for the service to be able to do something like that, that's so powerful. To be able to help a family finally find out where their child had been buried you know, from years ago.

Pete was there when the police came in and said they had a DNA match, and they interviewed Jebson. Pete set up the interview. It was a big deal for Wakefield.

We'd had so much flipping grief about this DNA testing, and we had prisoners who said they weren't gonna do it, but the law was that you could forcibly take a DNA test. And that's how they had their hair pulled out, because they were forcibly restrained and had follicles of their hair pulled out for DNA testing... or they used swabs in the mouth and took DNA tests. And it actually solved a crime.

Lisa was able to reassure there is support for staff, as well, in the form of a care team that is made up of people from different disciplines including psychologists, the governor etc.

'It's a matter of being there for that member of staff to talk.'

The care team could then direct people to more professional help if needed. Lisa indicated to us that there was no initial support before the care team existed. As we've previously mentioned, that support network was brought in again around the late 1990s. 'Before that, there was nothing. You'd go have a few drinks with your colleagues after work, that was it...'

Lisa's best friend committed suicide from the stress of working at Wakefield and it was horrendous.

'He was very popular, well known, and it affected quite a lot of the prisoners that knew him. They even clubbed together and bought some flowers that were sent to his funeral. They also sent cards.'

On the other hand, she said, some prisoners will send derogatory pictures and letters and are very anti-staff.

Staff still go to work, and they still do their job. They still walk in the footsteps of that member of staff. They're remarkable that way... You hear a lot from prisoners, you know, if they've got problems. Or if they get a 'Dear John' is the prime example – letter where the wife or the girlfriend is breaking off relationships.

On balance, we seemed to be receiving news of positive progress on both prisoner rehabilitation and staff care, and we were very glad to hear it.

Chapter 21

The Future

Britain's prison service is in crisis. Geoffrey Wansell remarked that 'Our jails are really full. The prison service is not in the modernisation business.'

We wanted to know from Jim how the prison service prepares prisoners for release. In particular, prisoners who were convicted at a young age for a long sentence and therefore haven't got much life experience prior to release. Often, prisoners being prepared for release are sent out via lower-level security prisons such as category D, or further easing them in through temporary releases.

He noted that the most important part when dealing with young people receiving a long sentence is to 'keep hope alive', echoing Hayley's words about hope and purpose, and to ensure they don't turn to harmful coping mechanisms, namely drugs or suicide. It's more difficult now than ever before due to these higher sentences and less experienced staff, who have not yet developed that necessary empathy whilst still being in charge, which takes years to develop.

He summarised that general sentencing periods for crimes has roughly doubled in recent years – where a crime that would have warranted ten years before now wields a sentence of twenty years. Due to this, many prisons are reaching capacity and struggling to retain staff, making an already difficult job even more difficult.

Geoffrey is well known for his views on whole-life terms. His 2022 book, *Pure Evil*, begins and ends with a balanced, incisive reflection on whole-life tariffs. It is compassionate from both a prisoner and a victim perspective.

As he said to us: 'I am pretty much convinced that whole-life terms do not represent any kind of deterrent. They don't deter serial killers. It is a pretty blunt weapon to lock up Jamie Reynolds for what could be sixty years.'

The case Geoffrey is referring to is that of one of the youngest people to be given a life term, which he is currently serving at Wakefield. At just twenty-three years of age, he killed his seventeen-year-old friend Georgia Williams. She was head girl of her school and a murder detective's daughter. Shopworker Reynolds, dubbed the 'Snuff Movie Killer' because of his obsession with violent pornography and the manner in which he killed Georgia, was only the forty-sixth person to be given a whole-life term when he was sentenced for his dreadful crime in December 2013.

He was apprehended in a Glasgow Premier Inn room three days after she vanished. Georgia's body was found in Wrexham woodland, about fifty miles from her house, on 31 May 2013. Reynolds was a shopworker but he knew Georgia as they were fairly close neighbours and had grown up in the same close-knit Telford community.

He manipulated her on the basis of their friendship into going to his home to assist him with a photo shoot. He lured her into posing for a photograph with her head in a noose before strangling her to death and having sex with her corpse. This violent, deviant behaviour convinced the judge that Reynolds had the potential to become a serial killer, part of the thinking underpinning the decision to hand him a whole-life tariff.

Whilst absolutely understanding the devastating tragedy losing a young girl in this hideous way is for her family, all of Geoffrey's work on balance has led him to the conclusion that 'fifty years is the most anyone should be incarcerated. I understand the feelings of the relatives, "he's taken my daughter's life", "he's taken my son's life", but the Scots at least have said, "no more than fifty years".'

However, Geoffrey recognises wholly the vast complexity of this topic, which can only ever be taken on a case-by-case basis.

'People are very complex. They can be brilliant at presenting. With someone like Ian Huntley, it is entirely possible he could pull the wool over people's eyes to get out and then reoffend, and then think about the likes of Ian Brady. There are such people as those who are pure evil, who do not accept any of the standards the rest of us live by.'

Geoffrey mused on the future as well as the past of Wakefield: 'Wakefield is simply geared for incarceration, not rehabilitation. Lock 'em up, leave 'em in the Monster Mansion. It doesn't represent any forward-thinking.'

* * *

At our second meeting, Vanessa was casually dressed and talked to us in a beautiful beamed study with exposed brickwork and a row of framed landscapes along a shelf behind her. As part of our follow-up conversation we wanted to talk to her about changes and the future. For Vanessa, it seems to be the awareness that many wrongful convictions have been made, coupled with her experience in the prison service, that has changed her opinion about the death penalty. As she elaborated:

> When I was younger, I was very anti-everything and had almost right-wing views, which you do when you meet the worst of society. My friends and I used to see child murderers and say, 'Bring back the death penalty.' As you get older you mellow more and you're not so petulant and so quick to judge. I rose up through the ranks. With that comes responsibility. You have to lead by example and see both sides.

Specifically, she started thinking about changing her views on the death penalty through the infamous 'Let him have it' case in the 1950s, when Derek Bentley was hanged. Bentley and Christopher Craig were cornered by the police in an attempted burglary. Bentley told Craig 'Let him have it', arguably meaning hand the gun to PC Miles. But he shot him. Craig, at sixteen, was too young to be hanged; however nineteen-year-old Bentley was old enough.

It was a great miscarriage of justice although Bentley was pardoned in 1993, but that was, of course, far too little too late. Vanessa didn't want to be responsible for killing someone who might later be proved innocent. It's not why she joined the prison service.

'What right do I have to take someone else's life? That's not my job.'

Lisa's extensive experience, too, has granted her very useful insights into how the prison system is changing. In her view, changes are being made by people 'in ivory towers' who don't actually know the prisons and are changing them for the worse rather than the better. They don't speak to staff to get their opinions.

That said, one amazing positive change was bringing in internal sanitation to cells to reduce the risk of suicide dramatically.

When asked to reflect on his more than three-decade long career, John explained that an ex-prisoner had reached out to him just weeks ago on LinkedIn. The message read:

Hi John, found you in a moment of reflection. Looks like you had a long career with the keys. You are one of the faces that I remember well and stood out as a decent and conscientious person amongst the long, hard journey. Thank you for that.

John likes to think that he has had that positive and reflective impact on many former prisoners, and that he has dedicated his life to helping and bettering people. As he summarises: 'Nobody forgets a good teacher. All I've ever wanted to do is to be a good teacher.'

Whilst he will never truly know the full extent and impact of his work, John hopes for a long-standing legacy that will be remembered for decades to come. To summarise his attitude to helping prisoners, John shared the speech that he would give to all new prisoners he worked with:

I will help and assist every one of you to make the best opportunities of your time in prison. Prison doesn't need to be a nasty place, and I will help and assist you. The prison rules and the laws in the prison's act are like bulrushes. I understand the regulations and the rules enough, I know which bulrushes I can pull back until they start creaking and the ones that if I touch them they will break in your hands. And I will use that expert knowledge and expertise in helping each one of you.

But, on the other side, that commitment and motivation, I will crawl over broken glass to nail anybody who I've found misbehaving and not conforming to the rules and regulations of my prison. You do something wrong, I will catch you, I will find out and I'll have you. Let's focus my commitment and enthusiasm in helping to assist you.

John's approach to his work and form of discipline was to believe that people have the potential to be better and to reform themselves, helping prisoners to understand that he was there to help and guide them. And that if that trust was broken, he would make the implications clear.

If it is in my gift to help and assist and improve people, then that's what I'll do, every day of the week.

Select Glossary
of Prison Slang
and Jargon

Prison has always had its own, very lively lexicon and code words, and these words have all echoed around the wings of Wakefield, including a few imports from the rich vocabulary of American prison slang.

All day: a life sentence

Bang up: locking a prisoner up in their cell, usually at night

Boss chair: a non-intrusive scanner, used in Wakefield, that can detect even tiny metal objects you might have secreted around or inside you

Box: solitary confinement

Diaper sniper: a child molester

E-man: a prisoner who has tried to escape

E wing: for inmates on their first night and induction

F wing: the wing for vulnerable prisoners, including paedophiles and rapists, the lowest of the low, who are segregated for their own protection

FLED: Full Licence Eligibility Date

Ghetto penthouse: the top tier of a cell block

Lifer: a prisoner serving a life sentence

Listener: a voluntary job undertaken by prisoners. Trained by the Samaritans, they are there to provide a listening ear to prisoners who may need it, at any time of the day or night

Mash: a mobile phone

Nick: prison

Nonce: a paedophile, also known as animals, bacon or bacon head

PO: Principal Officer

Porridge: increasingly old-fashioned term for serving your sentence, which can also sometimes be described by the associated slang word 'stir'

Potting: being covered in excrement

Prison wallet or prison purse: anal or vaginal storage unit for contraband, particularly drugs and mobile phones

Rabbit: a prisoner with a history of plotting to or attempting to escape

Ride with: to do favours, especially sexual favours, for another prisoner in exchange for protection or illicit items that have been smuggled in

ROTL: Release on Temporary Licence. Normally about a quarter of a way through their sentence, these prisoners can also go on home leave once they have passed their FLED (see above)

Screw: a prison officer

Shank: a knife or makeshift stabbing weapon

Snout: cigarettes or tobacco, which can effectively be one form of prison currency

SO: Senior Officer

Acknowledgements

Thank you to the fantastic, delightful and wise Ciara Lloyd, Publishing Director, Bonnier Books UK, and the amazing James Hodgkinson. Thanks, as always, to our incredible agents through the project, Matt Cole and Diane Banks at Northbank Talent Management, and to the ever-brilliant Martin Redfern for having faith in Monster Mansion from the beginning.

Heartfelt thanks to the wonderful Jaz Thompson, who gave up their evenings and weekends to gain us access to exceptional stories as a trusted, cerebral, responsible and curious book researcher.

Thanks to Roger French for offering support in every possible way throughout this writing process, and to Tim Leeman and Kevin Cooper, whose struggles against serious illness have offered inspiring examples of tenacity and courage. Thanks to Denise, Marie and Andy, Ged, Carmel, Sheila, Joy and Malcolm for love and support.

We often get asked how we don't end up killing each other when we are writing a book together. It sometimes seemed like we got closer to admission to Wakefield and New Hall ourselves during the stressful process of writing it, but we are very proud of the end product, and so very grateful to all our contributors, both named and anonymous, who made this book so raw, compelling and authentic.